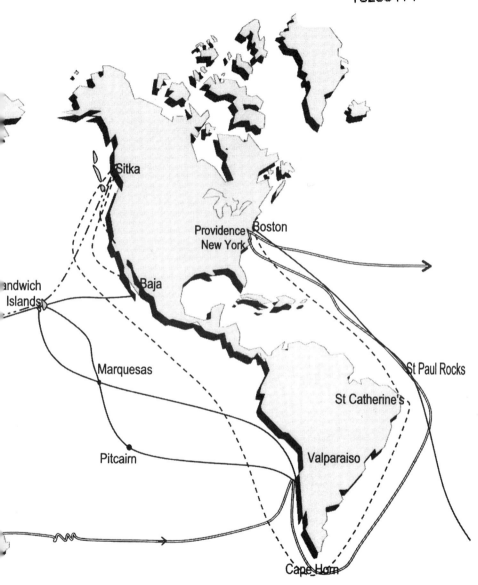

Sitka

Providence Boston
New York

Baja

andwich
Islands

Marquesas

St Paul Rocks

St Catherine's

Pitcairn

Valparaiso

Cape Horn

CALEB REYNOLDS

AMERICAN SEAFARER

Caleb Reynolds, 1771-1858

Alaska History No. 50

CALEB REYNOLDS

AMERICAN SEAFARER

Based on the papers of Caleb Reynolds, 1771-1858

by
EMILY REYNOLDS BAKER

Edited
by
RICHARD A. PIERCE

THE LIMESTONE PRESS
Kingston, Ontario : Fairbanks, Alaska
2000

U.S. Office:
The Limestone Press
c/o History Department
University of Alaska Fairbanks
Fairbanks, Alaska 99775-0860
U.S.A.

Distributed by University of Alaska Press.
P.O. Box 756240
Fairbanks, Alaska 99775-6240

International Standard Book Number 1-895901-25-1

Production: J. Ketz

Printed and bound in Canada by: Brown & Martin Limited
Kingston, Ontario

CONTENTS

ILLUSTRATIONS

PREFACE

My Grandmother's Love Affair

My grandfather's grandfather was a legend in our family. During holiday gatherings when fathers and uncles retired with their cigars after dinner, their talk, when they tired of politics, would turn to Caleb, the sea captain. They spoke of his adventurous life: sailing around "The Horn," trading with the King of Hawaii, and visiting Pitcairn Island and the H.M.S. *Bounty* mutineers.

When the logbooks and letters of Caleb Reynolds came into my grandfather's possession, I stood only a little taller then than the level of his desk, but I can see his bright eyes as he eagerly explored the logs. They were sent to him from New York City, where lived the last of his three maiden sisters, keeper of a collection guarded in the family for over 150 years. I remember the family's excitement for him. The real hand writing of his family-famous grandfather was in his hands at last.

In the meantime, my grandmother was equally interested in Caleb, and she too avidly perused the papers. But she, an amateur genealogist, was focused on tracing as many family lines as possible. And she couldn't trace Caleb. She had nothing to go on but the tradition that he had been orphaned at an early age and raised by an uncle in Maryland. She was determined to find that uncle, or some line of descent, or at least some record of Caleb's youth. The Reynolds men humored her, but were more interested in his adventures than in his parentage. As she talked about this mystery, she helped fan the flame of interest in me.

In one of Caleb's journals she found what appeared to be the date of his birth. He wrote in a margin: "C. Reynolds, b. October, 1771." On his protection paper he penciled "B. Maryland, R. Boston." In the 1930s she sent five dollars, a treasured amount then, for census records, locating only his last residence, Philadelphia. As she told and retold family stories, she always ended with Caleb, her real love affair.

I had grown up with the story, and when eventually his papers came to me, my assignment was clear: I must trace his path. The papers include ship's logs, youthful and ship-bound poetry, letters of instruction from his merchant owners, and, best of all, love letters to his wife. All are remarkably preserved and legible in a fine hand. They reveal a man of such character, and a life of such courage, that I sided with the men. The details of his parentage are a lesser matter.

Caleb Reynolds belongs on the list of America's least known and for the most part least heralded pioneers, the Boston fur traders of the Northwest Coast of America.

I began to know him well. My grandfather sat upon Caleb's knee, and I sat upon my grandfather's knee, so I was close to someone who knew him. Through his story, perhaps more will know of this great era of our history.

While this book is inspired by and based upon the writings of Caleb Reynolds, filling the gaps rested upon reading history. Researching the facts led me to marvelous book after amazing book, available to me from libraries coast to coast, and from purchases at museums and historical societies. One by one they revealed answers, and sometimes surprises.

They are carefully listed in the bibliography, but I have put their knowledge in my own words, adding to Caleb's, which are the words which tell the story.

ACKNOWLEDGEMENTS

Grateful thanks must go first to Mary Malloy, of Foxborough, Massachusetts, a recognized historian of the American maritime fur trade in the Pacific, who was well into her doctoral thesis on the subject when her name was given to me. When we spoke she exclaimed, "I've researched dozens of sources, but I never expected to find information in Nebraska!" And I never expected to find the enthusiastic encouragement, guidance and instant friendship she gave to me. Good fortune in finding people and facts has blessed me in this project, but none so providential as the introduction to Mary Malloy.

Mary in turn suggested I contact one of her mentors, Dr. Richard Pierce of the University of Alaska at Fairbanks History Department, and editor

ACKNOWLEDGEMENTS

of the Alaska History Series. Dr. Pierce engaged in a spirited correspondence with me after I first presented to him a sample of Caleb Reynolds' papers and an outline of his life. He has been a constant supporter of this project, offering guidance and encouragement at every turn.

The task of tracing this sea captain's path was absorbing, rewarding and educational. But putting it into a narrative was only part of what I envisioned. While I could produce a manuscript "camera ready" for the publisher, I wanted to be part of the design and illustration of the book production.

This achievement would never have come to pass without Frederika Eleanor ver Hulst. She came to assist me with her expertise in computer mechanics and stayed to fall in love with the project and the man, adding her creative imagination and talent to both content and illustration.

There were Evarts Fox and MacKinnon Simpson at the Hawaii Maritime Center in Honolulu who first deciphered for me the mysteries of the early phonetic spellings at the Sandwich Islands. The sea captains wrote what they heard the natives say, thus "Owyhee" for Hawaii (also the name of a river in Oregon). Another place name appears as "Tocaigh" and is actually Kawaihae. They helped with the task of learning about the islanders' then-unwritten language to discover where the ships were sailing.

There were many other very helpful staff members at the Oregon Historical Society in Portland, Oregon; the Lahaina Historical Society in Maui, Hawaii; the Library of Congress in Washington, D.C.; the Peabody Museum in Salem, Massachusetts; the Bancroft Library of the University of California in Berkeley; and last but not least those at the Swanson and Clark Libraries in Omaha, Nebraska.

The transcription of Caleb Reynolds' papers was at most times a pleasure, due to his handsome, unusually legible hand. But thanks to Aunt Charlotte Reynolds Linsert and cousin Lois Jarzynka Reynolds, many of his letters and poems were instantly readable in their typewritten transcripts.

ACKNOWLEDGEMENTS

Laura Chilton Reynolds bound these pages in several copies for all remaining descendants, that they might be introduced to the man.

But these fine sources are only a part of the collection. No one ever transcribed his three ship's logs, two long poems, and other important documents. His handwriting remained a marvel even in the ship logs, so thanks go also to Captain Caleb Reynolds himself.

In all letters, poetry, and log entries, his spelling, punctuation and syntax are respected as written. I have eschewed the use of "sic" and hope the reader will forgive what appears to be strange or erroneous spelling and style. At the same time, they may enjoy translating "Onnarooroo" to Honolulu, and savor the language of the era.

Emily Reynolds Baker

CHAPTER ONE

The "Boston Men"

"... My native shore, adieu.
Auspicious blows the parting gale,
With willing hand I trim the sail ... "

On a foggy New England evening in early September, 1804, the ship *Pearl* of Boston, a three-masted square rigger of 200 tons, 10 guns, John Ebbets, captain, raised anchor and stood out of Boston Harbor, bound for the other side of the world.

Her assignment was to proceed south around Cape Horn and northward on the Pacific Ocean to the Northwest Coast of America, there to seek the fur pelts of the sea otter from the island natives, to carry this cargo to Canton in China, and there to trade them for tea, silk, and porcelain.

It would take the *Pearl* six months to reach her destination at Nootka Sound, on the west coast of Vancouver Island, and almost three years to complete her task.

In Ebbets' crew of twenty-two was Caleb Reynolds, an American seaman, sailing as third mate. His apprentice log recorded that in two hours the fog had lifted, in two days the ship was abreast of Bermuda, and in two months she was crossing the Equator. Reynolds' log described the crossing:

> "Remarks 5 November, 1804—
>   ... the crew heartily employed in performing
> those ceremonies and rites that Custom, by length
> of time, has established at crossing the Equator."

It is likely he was among those crewmen who were making a first Equator crossing, paying obeisance to King Neptune in the pageant famous among mariners to this day.

Aboard the *Pearl*, Caleb Reynolds was part of one of America's great adventure stories: the trading ships of turn-of-the-century Boston, seeking their fortune in the North Pacific and China.

Since 1787, Boston ships had appeared in the Pacific on this brave adventure in increasing numbers.

Long before the land-based American settlers surged westward across the vast new land, the band of sea-going Americans had reached the far west side of the continent, taking not the well-known route around the Cape of Good Hope, but the more dangerous route south then west around the dreaded Cape Horn into the Pacific Ocean.

The story begins as the American war for independence ends.

Merchants of the new nation were freed by their new independence and by the continuing war between France and England to sail where they liked and to trade as they wished. And they needed trade, especially with China, for that valuable commodity, tea, if not for silk and porcelain. They hadn't the silver or gold used by the British and Spanish, but what could they offer? They had to find a medium of trade.

Fiercely independent and self-sufficient, China had few wants or needs. Furthermore, the British, and perhaps some Americans, thought America, without foreign possessions affording ports for rest, could never hope to establish its own trade. But it was the great British explorer James Cook who had shown the way.

First, Cook had discovered the mid-Pacific islands he called the "Sandwich Islands," the providential rest stop of "Owyhee." Those islands, on the route from the Northwest Coast to Canton, providing rest, water and provisions, made the long voyages possible.

Second, Cook's crew discovered the trade medium needed. Shivering in the icy north, they found that mere buttons and beads bought warm furs from willing natives at Nootka

Sound. Later, much to their surprise, they discovered their fur clothing, even makeshift, worn and dirty, was so desired in Canton it was worth many times the beads and trinkets that had bought it. For this was not mere fur, this was the pelt of the sea otter, sometimes six feet long and three feet wide, the most luxurious fur of the Northwest Coast waters, perhaps of any waters.

Many of Cook's crewmen were quick to see this trade potential. James King, who took command after Cook's death, wrote that the "rage" with which his seamen were possessed to make their fortunes was close to mutiny.

One such crewman was John Ledyard, an American in the employ of the British Navy on Cook's ship. The fur experience burned in his mind as Cook's ships arrived in England in 1780. Two years later, when he returned to America, Ledyard wrote an account of Cook's third voyage. Though unauthorized, it appeared in 1783, the first American book published about the Northwest Coast.

By the time the official account came from London in 1785, word of the Northwest fur trade was well circulated in America and in France and Spain as well. Various merchants pondered, but for a time abandoned, the prospect of entering the trade. Interestingly, Ledyard would be instrumental in putting Boston in the game.

Determined to be the first American to round Cape Horn and reach the Coast, Ledyard obtained the backing of financier Robert Morris of Philadelphia, but could find no ship or crew. Ships and money were scarce in the postwar era, and just as important, mariners were loathe to consider the perils of Cape Horn. Postwar conditions were difficult everywhere. There was as yet no semblance of a nation, and new states even set tariffs against each other.

Still, the China trade was a necessary objective. A group of merchant investors, including Morris, finally launched the first American ship to trade in Canton. She was the *Empress of China*, truly an American ship, with investors from Baltimore, Philadelphia, New York and

Salem, and a Bostonian as supercargo or chief trader. She carried a cargo of ginseng, a product known to be popular in China for renewed vigor, even a "dose for immortality." The *Empress* went eastward around the Cape of Good Hope and returned the same way. Canton accepted the *Empress'* ginseng and rewarded her with the all-important tea, silk and porcelain.

Meantime, Ledyard took a letter of introduction from Robert Morris to New England, but again failing to find ships, he went to Paris. Here his letter and the fact of his being an American gained him a meeting with Benjamin Franklin, who in turn introduced him to the salon of Thomas Jefferson, just then assuming the post of ambassador to France.

Jefferson was taken by Ledyard's enthusiasm for trade and settlement on the Northwest Coast, and added those ideas to his own. He even encouraged Ledyard's amazing intention to get to Nootka Sound by *walking* across Russia, and sailing from there across the Pacific to the Northwest Coast. From there Ledyard planned to walk eastward across our unexplored western lands to Virginia. He actually started on this quest, but was stopped in Russia by the wary Empress Catherine.

Another American was listening to those Paris conversations, a young architecture student named Charles Bulfinch. He was not likely to have his mind on world trade, rather on his tour of the great buildings of Europe. But once home in Boston, joining his father and other merchants such as Joseph Barrell of Boston, Bulfinch brought reports of the talk in Paris and helped persuade his father to invest in a plan. Barrell, a shrewd businessman like Morris, had contributed ginseng to the successful *Empress* cargo and was anxious for further trade. The enthusiasm of investors of New York and Philadelphia had cooled after experiencing the expenses, fees, and graft in Canton, but Boston was not discouraged. She had less to offer in trade than either New York or Philadelphia, who had large crops and manufactured items, and furs looked like the answer to her problems. Boston took the challenge to conquer the feared route around the Horn and go for the fur. Together with partners, Barrell sent the first Boston ships around the Horn to the Coast.

They sent two vessels, with captains John Kendrick and Robert Gray in the ship *Columbia* and the sloop *Lady Washington*. It was September, 1787, the American Constitution only just signed, when they departed. In spite of delays and difficult encounters in the North Pacific, by July 1789 they had sufficient cargo for Canton. For reasons unknown, the two captains traded ships. Gray sailed the *Columbia* to Canton, sold his cargo of furs, and returned by way of the Cape of Good Hope, the first American skipper to circumnavigate the globe. When he reached Boston in August, 1790, others quickly seized upon the idea of sending more ships and men to the Northwest Coast.

Although British and Spanish traders had tested the northern waters, as did a few ships from America's other cities, in a short two or three years the Bostonians dominated the scene. Soon the natives' word for American white men was "Boston men."

On his second voyage Robert Gray discovered, named, and claimed for America the great Columbia River. Its wide and treacherous bar had caused earlier explorers such as Vancouver and Meares to miss the river. Here fur trading history would be made and western settlers by way of the sea would make the coast their own.

When the *Pearl* rounded Cape Horn and Caleb Reynolds' log charted her position at Longitude 100 degrees West and Latitude 47 *South*, another band of Americans also reached 100 degrees West, resting on the banks of the Missouri River. Lewis and Clark matched the *Pearl*'s western position, though marking their latitude at 47 *North*. The settlers by land would soon catch up, but it was the mariners of America who first reached the west coast.

CHAPTER TWO

Ship *Pearl*
1804-1807

"I sing Pacific Isles, congenial clime . . .
Here void of care a happy people stray,
Enjoy their fruits and sport their time away."

The *Pearl* beat her way around Cape Horn, in the southern summer, but at latitude so far south as to flirt with ice and to sail where the winds and currents of two oceans clashed, the place mariners called the most dangerous, difficult passage in any part of the world. The *Pearl* made this passage on Christmas, 1804: The ship's log reported heavy seas and violent gales on Christmas Eve, and first mate John Suter wrote,

"This being Christmas Day, fresh food . . . Squalls and gales but ship making no water."

Clear of the Horn, they sailed north by west and approached the island of Hawaii. Six months and half a world away from Boston, the tired crew found fresh water, food, and a brief tropical rest.

As third mate, Reynolds kept a log, in which he reported that they were welcomed "by native canoes in large numbers, bringing fruit," while the ship worked with difficulty against wind and tide to find anchorage at "Tocaigh" Bay, on the northwest shore of Hawaii. "John Young came on board and accompanied us south to Karakakooa."

These places on the leeward side of the island of Hawaii are Kawaihae and Kealakekua Bay. Kawaihae, which Reynolds calls "Tocaigh," was the site of the King's sacred temple or heiau and his favorite residence. It was also the home of John Young, the King's trader.

While anchored in thirteen fathoms at Kealakekua Bay, the *Pearl*'s officers and crew en-

gaged in cleaning the ship's side, filling and stow-
ing casks of water, buying vegetables and hogs
and making various repairs to the rigging. On
March 8th, 1805, "all hands were sent ashore to
take the land air," to return at evening. Then
after less than two weeks they returned John
Young to his home and departed for Nootka
Sound on Vancouver Island. They arrived at that
appointed place of business in April 1805.

These northern waters were the home of
the sea otter, whose fur, the thickest in the
world, was so coveted in Canton. Otter fur
was described by William Sturgis, famous sea
captain and shipper: ". . . excepting a beautiful
woman and a lovely infant . . . it is . . . the
most attractive natural object that can be
placed before me."

A Bostonian's hunt did not mean finding,
killing and skinning the creatures. Rather, he
sought Northwest Coast natives and canoes,
which emerged from shore, coming alongside
to offer pelts and bartering for the white man's
curiosities. To gather enough Canton cargo,

the *Pearl* worked the summer of 1805 and stayed in the islands the long winter and another summer.

They traded port to port, spending sixteen months navigating between the dozens of forested, sometimes hostile islands which stretch many miles from Vancouver Island past the Queen Charlotte Islands to Sitka. What a contrast to the Pacific paradise of Hawaii! But neither the apprentice nor the mate's log described these thickly forested shorelines, the hill after hill leading to mountain after snow-covered mountain. Their eyes were on the water, watching for the native canoes.

Caleb Reynolds had come to this voyage rather older than the average seaman on a first assignment. Issued at Baltimore in 1801, his protection paper reads:

"An American seaman, aged twenty-seven Years or thereabouts, of the Height of five feet, eight inches, having a ruddy Complexion, dark Eyes, common Nose, dark brown Hair, small Mouth, has a scar on his left ear, one on his right hand, and one of his left knee, has this day produced to me Proof in the Manner directed in the Act, entitled 'An Act for the Relief and Protection of American Seamen' and pursuant to the said act I do hereby Certify that the said Caleb Reynolds is a Citizen of the United States of America."

While Boston was home port to the *Pearl's* merchant managers, J. & T. Lamb, Caleb's home had been Maryland, where family tradition says he was orphaned at a young age and raised by an uncle. Born on the eve of the American Revolution, he grew up in turbulent times. No writings exist to describe his growing years but for some youthful poetry, a craft which became his lifelong interest. Copied into a small journal which says that they had been published in Boston, the poems give evidence of a good education, an intelligent mind and a sensitive nature. They include odes to American presidents as well as verses about friendship, loyalty and lovely ladies. A verse about leaving the land provides his only autobiographical statement:

"In life's first dawn I strayed
Till fortune took me to the main;
With luring hope of ampler gain,
My thoughtless heart obeyed . . ."

Hundreds of America's men entered a life at sea by "fortune" for "ampler gain." The merchant sea trade was a successful and important business, but the seaman's job was hard work and not romantic except for the chance to see the world. Some men would find a lifetime career; others would earn enough to buy a farm back home.

Caleb Reynolds was one of those who learned at sea to become a ship's captain.

By the time the *Pearl* reached the Northwest Coast in 1805 she was one of dozens of American ships trading in and out of the faraway islands. No less daring or dangerous than a decade before, the three-year voyage had become the norm, and the fur trade was at its height.

Built at Milton, Massachusetts in 1803, the *Pearl* was barely 12 feet deep. She had two decks, three masts, a square stern, no galleries, a scroll figurehead. Such small ships, traveling alone at sea, were very small homes for crews of twenty or so men, cargoes of barreled water, beef and salt pork, live hogs purchased and butchered along the way, and the lumber, iron, sailcloth and other supplies needed by the armorer, carpenter and crew, but they were the preferred size for maneuvering among the islands.

A ship's outbound cargo also included items chosen for barter to lure natives' capricious tastes. Scarcely two years after the first "Boston men" arrived in the *Columbia*, the Indians became harder to please. The beads and trinkets of James Cook's men were long out of favor, and the next traders, encountering differences in taste from tribe to tribe, began to improvise. Men would strip their clothes of buttons or even sell a whole coat. One captain tried offering women's garments made from sailcloth. Forges were fired up aboard ship to fashion things of iron—chisels, files, daggers, or jewelry such as iron collars or bracelets. Copper or brass pots were much desired, and gladly given for the precious fur. By the next voyage perhaps none of these would please. The day came when muskets and powder were demanded, bringing inevitable trouble. The traders would give what the natives would take.

There were fierce encounters and savage attacks. There were crew desertions and mutinies from stress, dwindling food and hard work; some captains were selfish or unreasonable. There were rigging accidents and occasional pirating to cope with, and also, always, the weather. All these conditions were accepted for the importance of the prize: commerce with China.

The *Pearl* and her voyages appear in many histories of the period. The manuscript of the official log of this 1804-7 voyage is preserved at the Massachusetts Historical Society in Boston, and presents very difficult handwriting, illegible entries and strange spelling of ordinary words as well as of place names. In facts-only fashion, it records the visits of canoes with "got some skins" without, alas, telling us what was traded.

Suter, Ebbets' first mate and supercargo, was famous for the take of skins on this voyage, but not for the clarity of his log. F. W. Howay, authority on maritime history, wrote that this log "wins the prize for illegibility." Suter of course wrote hurriedly; he was busy making amazing trades.

Meantime Reynolds was keeping his log, and what can be read is in his fine, clear hand. Carefully preserved for almost two hundred years in possession of his descendants, three of Reynolds' ship's logs survive, but the *Pearl* log only in spite of a mysterious seven-inch circle burned through its two-inch thickness. The damage, as old as the book, makes legible only the top and bottom page entries. What remains in the scorched shards suffices only to give dates and nautical positions, and a few references to Hawaii and points west. This log might have lent more detail or anecdote, given Reynolds' occasional departure from official log language, but any such remarks are lost.

But he did provide anecdote, as the poet in him was also at work. The *Pearl* had on board a ship's dog, who one day during the first long summer on the Northwest Coast put the crew into a scramble. Reynolds recorded it in poetry.

"The death of Gunner, an unfortunate Ship-Dog, who in a fit of canine madness jumpt overboard, on the 29th of August, 1805, from the Ship Pearl of Boston, in Tates Kei on the Northwest

Coast of America, and expired in that element, which in similar cases has been resorted to as a sovereign antidote. Together with the human exertions of little Quixote to restore him to life.

"Relate, oh Muse, the sad disastrous night:
Our dog ran mad and put the watch to flight,
How to the steerage, some in haste withdrew,
And others bounding to the cabin flew;
How some like squirrels, on the rigging treed,
By prudence to elude his speed.

Poor Gunner! in the maze of phrenzy hurl'd,
Now tumbled headlong to the watery world,
Now little Quixote heard our frantic cries,
Scratched his round head and ope'd his eager eyes,
Rose from his couch, by generous instinct flew;
Derides the tardy and exhorts the crew,
To purchase glory midst alarm and strife
And snatch the sinking victim back to life.

Quick o'er the stern, with lucky speed he sprung,
And gained the boat, which by her moorings hung;
And from the waves the lifeless body took,
With sighs and grunts the dripping carcass shook.
We drew him lifeless from the fatal tide,
By ropes suspended from the sable side;
On the cold deck he lay, without a shroud
Expos'd to every eye, and all the crowd,
Til morn, returning, cheer'd the orient sky,
Saw the last rite, and heard each parting sigh.

Ah hapless dog! from Boston to the main,
Impell'd by gratitude, and not by gain,
A youthful master's steps and toils to wait
To share his fortune, or to meet his fate.
Thus on an ample coast to find no grave,
But the cold ooze beneath the sullen wave.
For dogs, and puppies, though of humble note,
Here first my bashful Muse distends her throat;
And haply should she gain but low applause,
She yet may chant in some sublimer cause,
May raise her notes, and bear on bolder wings
The cum'brous fame of senators and kings;
Or, wake in passive breasts the patriots' flame
And touch bold arrogance with decent shame."

By 5 August 1806 *Pearl* had departed the Northwest Coast to return to Hawaii.

"Remarks 3 Sept. 1806—anchor Tocaigh Bay, John Young on board. 6 Sept.—Saw Brig *Lady*, Capt. Hall—King visits with wives; 20 Sept.—bot hogs and vegetables; 21 Sept.—Island of Woahoo with Whyteete Bay—saw Winship in *O'Cain*. 24 Sept.—Had King and all on board, bot hogs from King. 25 Sept.—Starboard watch on liberty; 26 Sept.—Larboard watch on liberty.

"Remarks 28 Sept.—depart for Canton, the people engaged in salting pork and cleaning skins. *Perseverance*, Capt. Delano in company."

The *Pearl* spent only a few days in Hawaii en route north in March, 1805, but the poet's interest in the "Elysian greens" was not forgotten. What sailor, worlds away from home, and enjoying for the first time the beauty and respite of these verdant islands would not rhapsodize? Reynolds began to fill a journal of forty-two pages in which he penned an ode revealing in praise and wonder his discovery and study of the history and customs of the islands of 1806. It begins:

> "I sing pacific Isles, congenial clime,
> Here Nature triumphs in eternal prime.
> Here varied hill and vale her fruits adorn
> And pour their fragrance on the scented morn.
> Here op'ning blooms and rip'ning fruits appear,
> And joyous plenty crowns the circling year."

At the Sandwich Islands Reynolds met two giants of Pacific history, the great King Kamehameha and his advisor, John Young. Young was an Englishman aboard the New York ship *Eleanora*, which arrived at the Hawaiian Islands under command of Captain Simon Metcalf in 1790. Accidentally left behind in Hawaii, he became a trusted friend, tutor, and translator to King Kamehameha, who made him Governor of Hawaii. Young's knowledge of guns and warfare was valuable to the royal goals: the King defeated the other island chiefs to become absolute ruler of the Sandwich Islands by 1795.

On September 28, 1806, the *Pearl* departed Hawaii for Canton, reaching Macao November 8 and proceeding to Whampoa and then Canton. The record of their arrival is dismissed with "Ebbets went up to Canton." Only a captain went ashore, and only to visit the riverside factories, never beyond. While the Chinese welcomed American ships and trade, no one was allowed to enter the city of Canton, much less the Chinese interior. Trading was handled in a complicated, time-consuming manner, with plenty of tariffs, fees, commissions and graft, making it expensive as well. The process might take two or three months, even though American agencies were established there to act on behalf of the traders. The scene was colorful and interesting, as carved and decorated Chinese boats plied the river. In this year of 1805-6, Chinese imports were over five million dollars, and American vessels brought out ten million pounds of tea!

While the *Pearl* awaited the completed trades and welcomed Chinese merchants aboard to examine the skins, the crew was able to buy bread, coffee and other food from nearby ships. A partial report on the primary purchases in Suter's log reads:

> "50 chests Hyson, 120 bales tea, 24 boxes silks, 5 boxes silks, 350 packages nankeens, 313 bundles nankeens, 33 cases silks."

Her trading done, the *Pearl* left Canton in January, 1807, sailing down the South China Sea, with the *Jefferson* of Philadelphia in company. To make the trip home she would encounter the danger of shoals, reefs and tough currents en route to Java for provisions, then navigate the treacherous rocks of the Straits of Sunda, en route to the Indian Ocean. Once there, a ship would make for the Cape of Good Hope and then Boston.

Crossing the Indian Ocean, Reynolds wrote:

"The Homeward Bound Passage
Ship Pearl at sea, 1807

"As nearing still our native shore,
And half our toils and dangers o'er,
Still keeling Ocean's wide domain,
With joy elate, each hardy swain
Impatient flies to set the sail,
Full crowding in the eastern gale,
Till Green Hesperia's hills in view
Shall lure the sail and cheer the crew.

Now our chief, observant stands,
The octant waving in his hands:
Through level'd tube directs his sight
And careful scans the solar height,
Marks each gradation as we roll,
Recede, or gain upon the pole.
The point we hold, still as we stay,
Progressing o'er the trackless way.

Near full three circuits has the sun
Rotative through the eliptic run,
Since from that shore, with fav'ring gales
We weighed our anchors, loos'd our sails.
Hesperia's hills, then from our sight
Soon veil'd their verdant tops in night.
Now o'er the chart, with skillful hand
He marks the course toward the land
As taught by geometric lore
The distance to the viewless shore,

Then points the way, and trims the sail,
Nice balanced in the fresh'ning gale.

Ah then, what bosom heaved a sigh
Or turned toward the shore, and eye
In steadfast gaze, in fond adieu,
Til Ocean closed the aching view
And raised to heav'n a silent prayer
That heaven would guard some weeping fair."

After the "near full three circuits" of the sun, the *Pearl* arrived opposite Cape May, New Jersey, on May 10, 1807.

CHAPTER THREE

Ship *Isabella*
1809-1812

" . . . Two peaceful nations, on this festive day,
Unfurl and bid their standards play . . . "

Once again on shore in May, 1807, Reynolds waited two years for another assignment, confined to the land along with other American shippers and crews under the Jefferson Embargo. Britain and France were at war and both were impressing men from the merchant ships.

Only a few ships cleared Boston in that summer and fall to beat the embargo deadline.

Ebbets' *Pearl* profits must have been successful, for supercargo John Suter was quickly made captain of the *Pearl*, which was fitted out in unusual haste for another voyage to the Coast. This time Suter took to Canton the largest cargo of fur then on record, 6,000 skins. These, with additional cargo of sandalwood, were worth over $150,000, which sold at auction in Boston, after expenses, for over $200,000.

By the time Suter had returned to Boston for this 1810 auction, Reynolds was again at sea. But their paths would cross again in future adventures to China.

During the two years of the embargo the Mariner Reynolds' employment activity is unknown, but the Poet Reynolds left a record of contacts in various Massachusetts towns where he was posted, such as Billerica, Lexington and Canton. His poems reflect a busy social life and many interests, including politics. He was in Pelham, New Hampshire, when he penned an ode for Madison's inauguration, and another for Jefferson.

"For Mr. Jefferson's retiring from office:
Behold the sage, the wise and great
This day retires from cares of State
To Monticello's calm retreat
There blest amidst his ample shades
Where no ambitious scheme invades
Where all the Muses meet.
Honor attends the patriot there
For him a nation breathes her prayer;
'May Heaven thy joys increase'.
No greater joy could warm that breast
Than but to see a world at rest
From war, to arts of peace."

When the embargo was finally lifted, the Boston company of Boardman and Pope sent the *Isabella* to "the Coast" and hired Reynolds as second officer under Captain William Heath Davis.

"It is agreed upon between Boardman and Pope & the owners of the Ship *Isabella* and Caleb Reynolds, second officer of said ship, who has signed articles to proceed in that capacity in said ship on her present intended voyage to the North West Coast of America and elsewhere on a trading voyage and thence to Canton, backwards and

forwards until her return to the United States.
That for his services as second officer of said ship
of every name and nature during the voyage he
shall receive twelve dollars per month wages, and
one percent of the net proceeds of the said ship's
cargo at the close of the voyage in Boston. But no
privilege to be allowed him nor any trade of any
kind during the voyage.

> "Boston, June 5, 1809, Boardman and Pope,
> Agents;
> Witness, Robt P. Williams; Signed, Caleb
> Reynolds"

At Boston Light in June, 1809, knowing this
time how far the voyage would take him,
Reynolds wrote, in part:

> *"Ye less'ning hills, awest that lie,*
> *In ether mixt with yon dim sky,*
> *My native shore, adieu.*
> *Auspicious blows the parting gale,*
> *With willing hand I trim the sail,*
> *But turn to gaze on thee . . ."*

At the typical trading-vessel size of 209 tons,
the *Isabella* set out for the Northwest Coast,
around the Horn for the Pacific. Unlike the

Pearl, which traded for sixteen months along the Northwest Coast, the *Isabella* roamed north and south along the California coast between June, 1810 and September, 1811, returning to New Archangel at Norfolk Sound.

The story of the *Isabella*'s 1810 voyage is prominent in histories of the maritime era. Notable among them is the manuscript, *Solid Men of Boston*, held at the Bancroft Library in Berkeley, California. The author, William D. Phelps, "had the honor of commanding the ship *Atahualpa*, outfitted by Bryant and Sturgis."

Based upon the journals or logs of Jonathan Winship and his brother Nathan, who formed a partnership with William Heath Davis, *Solid Men* includes stories about the *Isabella* and Russia's Alexander Baranov. Reynolds, serving with Captain Davis, was thus introduced not only to Davis but also to the Winship brothers, active in the Pacific since 1805. And he met the Russians.

Russian trading on the Coast had been increasing for sixty years. Their settlement became official in 1799 with the Tsar's appointment of Alexander Baranov as governor for the Russian-American Company at New Archangel in Norfolk Sound, now Sitka and Sitka Sound.

While they sought more territory for Mother Russia and gradually moved along the coast of California as far south as Fort Ross, the Russians were barred from trading in Canton. Governor Baranov was therefore glad to make deals with the Americans, trading pelts for European manufactures, such as ammunition, sugar, wines and spirits. American ships were a closer source of supply than the Russians' mother country, and the Russians were willing to trade their furs. Naturally, Baranov put on welcoming parties, and *Solid Men* says "the practice of sociability was to not break up the party until all were drunk."

The pelts the Russians offered in return for European goods were hunted and produced by the Aleut and Kodiak natives, long the serfs of the Russians. An enterprising American, Joseph O'Cain, saw the potential of hiring natives-plus-canoes from the Russians, enabling him to seek sea otter as far south along the Spanish coast as Baja California.

Soon after the *Isabella* arrived on the Coast, Reynolds' old friend John Ebbets appeared, in command of the *Enterprise*, bringing supplies to Norfolk Sound from John Jacob Astor. Already controlling most of the fur trade in America's interior, Astor had ventured into the maritime fur trade. In 1811 he established a trading post at Astoria at the mouth of the Columbia River, but he was not the first with this idea. *Solid Men* records that Jonathan Winship investigated the idea two years earlier, but found the Chinook Indians so hostile that "with feelings of a devout and manly heart" he abandoned the idea, not wanting to shed the blood of both Indians and Americans.

Now Captain Davis entered the sea otter game. Contracting "O'Cain style" with the Russians Golovnin and Rikord, he hired a gang of Aleuts with forty-eight "bidarkys," or canoes, with a Russian commander, took them aboard, and set off to roam the coast of California. Reynolds' journal notes: "Dimensions of the canoe, or bydarky, of Kodiac: Length 20 feet, breadth 2 feet 6 inches. Made of skins, they are light weight but strong."

It was in the Farallon Islands opposite San Francisco that Davis encountered the veteran Winship brothers in the ships *O'Cain* and *Albatross*. Using the O'Cain system in a deal with Russians on shares, the Winships with their one hundred and fifty Aleuts and seventy to eighty canoes were sealing and stealing, going within ninety miles of the Spanish coast. Sea otters, being depleted in the north, were to be found here, and seals aplenty. With the Winships, Davis and the *Isabella* risked poaching, sometimes with cooperation of the Spanish, sometimes not. *Solid Men* says the three captains became known as "Lords of the Pacific."

In August the captains returned to New Archangel and engaged themselves in sociability. Here Baranov commissioned Reynolds to write a poem for a Commercial Festival. The traders were celebrating their mutual successes.

"The following lines were written on and for the 3rd of August, 1810, a day appointed by His Excellency Alexander Berrenof Knight of the Order of St. Ann, and Governor of the Russian American Company, Captain Gollovin of the Imperial Russian Navy, Capt. Ebbetts of New York, and Captain William H. Davis of Boston for a Commercial Festival, and read by Captain Davis at the sitting.

"Lured by the lights, which cheering Commerce shed,
From diff'rent realms, by lib'ral motives led,
Two peaceful nations, on this festive day
Unfurl and bid their joyous standards play.
Long may this confidence, its powers extend,
And every wish and every interest blend;
Nor shall Ambition from his bloodstain'd car
Hoodwink and drive them to destructive war!

"Here honored Berrenoff, who toils to lead
An infant State beneath his guardian care,
With generous Gollovin, toucht with the flame
Of sacred friendship and enlightened fame,
And young Columbia's sons, who stretch their sails
O'er polar waves, in equatorial gales,
Meet in full concord, speech and customs blend,
Confirm their confidence, their trade extend."

One can almost see the glasses raised. The poem must have pleased the assembly, for a few days later at another gathering Reynolds presented the long poem about the Sandwich Islands, "*The Sailor's Elysium*," which he had begun aboard the *Pearl* on his first view of Hawaii. The poem extols the land, the people and the history of the islands, and shows Reynolds to have been a thorough student of island traditions and agriculture, while he romanticized the telling. A typical stanza appears here under his title:

"A Poem wrote during a short stay at the Island of Owyhee, by an American sailor, then engaged in a voyage from Boston round the world."

See all the fruits of every climate grace
The sloping surface to the sea-worn base;
Here void of care a happy people stray,
Enjoy their fruits and sport their time away.
No frigid blasts, no cold autumnal rain
Check the crude year nor disappoint the swain;
No wasting cares his present joys arrest
No cold suspicions harbor in his breast . . .

In stanzas of iambic pentameter, interspersed with explanatory notes, the *Elysium* survives in an inch-thick bound journal, forty-two pages when transcribed in today's printing. It received the group's admiration, for on the journal's end pages appears an astonishing impromptu "order form," wherein seventeen "Nor'westmen" signed their names, requesting copies of the long poem, some asking for twenty! They include Baranov, Winship, and Davis.

The page of signatures and orders begins in the handwriting of one of the signers:

"Captain Gollovin & Lieutenant Rickard of H. I. Russian Majesty's ship Diana, by particular favor of the Author Mr. Renald, had perused with mental pleasure the manuscript of his truly interesting Poem "The Sailor's Elysium" request that the following number of Copies of it might be sent them to Russia by Captain Wm. Davis's favor, who with his wonted civilities has offered his services on this occasion.

"To be directed on Capt. Gollovin's or Rickard's name, to the directors of the Russian American Company in St. Petersbourg."

Headed south again in September, the *Isabella* headquartered in Bodega Bay north of San Francisco. The canoes crept into inlets around San Francisco Bay, not undetected by the commandante but nevertheless successful in gathering thousands of skins. Not an otter was safe, and the *Isabella* took almost three thousand otter. Meanwhile the Winships stowed over five thousand skins. So it was a large share for Baranov— his part of eight thousand skins—that the three ships could present to him when they went once more to Norfolk Sound.

On this visit some of the men enjoyed the respite of a trip to the hot springs outside Sitka, and Reynolds described their excursion:

Sitka, September 4, 1811
    Journal of a party to the hot Springs, consisting of Capts. Davis and Winship, Messrs. Clark and Caldwell, myself and the boat's crew.
    ... We landed a little after sunset on the 5th in a heavy fall of rain, opposite the Spring ... we found there two small houses, and on the beach a decent tent for our reception which had been put

up by order of the Gov'r. While the fire was kindling to prepare our supper, we spread our beds in the best possible manner, which by this time had got considerable wet, and ourselves very chilly, whereupon I jumped into the pool, which was large and warm. The contrast produced the most delightful sensation; after bathing and putting on dry flannels took supper, and slept comfortably through the night.

. . . We followed the stream to where it gushed out from the side of the mountain . . . where the water was hot enough to boil an egg. We made the experiment on fish and turnips, which succeeded well.

. . . On the salubrious properties of this Spring we cannot speak with much certainty: In the first place there was not an invalid among us, and secondly the constant bad weather we had, and wet and uncomfortable lodging, might have been an equal drawback on what might have been.

. . . The only effect I could observe produced on myself was relaxation, and the healing of some small eruptions and sores on the skin. Yet I believe these waters will be found beneficial in cases of the Rheumatism and cramp, also eruptions and diseases of the skin.

. . . Our stay at the Spring was three nights
and two days; we left it on the morning of the 8th,
with fine light wind and clear weather.

Two months later, en route to Hawaii,
Reynolds wrote on the end-paper of his journal,

"Ship *Isabella*, at Sea November 14, 1811—
Bet a suit of clothes with Captain William H.
Davis that the net proceeds of our present voyage would not exceed 120 thousand dollars, myself in the affirmative."

At Hawaii the "Lords of the Pacific" bar-
tered with King Kamehameha to augment their
cargo of seventy-five thousand skins with a
supply of sandalwood, which was fast becoming the coveted commodity for the China
trade.   King Kamehameha, recognizing the
potential of his sandalwood, had put a taboo on
all the island trees, making cutting and trading
a royal monopoly.   Shrewdly, the "Lords"
persuaded the King to sign an exclusive ten-
year contract with them for all the trade of his

fragrant wood, the King to receive one quarter of the profits from China.

By the end of December, 1811, the three ships sailed for China. But before their negotiations in China were finished, America was at war with Britain, and English ships blockaded the China coast and the Sandwich Islands.

Suddenly Caleb Reynolds' path twisted. On the 19th of April, 1812, he was "regularly discharged" from the *Isabella.*

> "American Consulate, Canton
>
> "I, John P. Cushing, Consular Agent for the United States of America at Canton, certify that Caleb Reynolds is a Native Citizen of this United States of America and that he has been regularly discharged from the American Ship *Isabella,* in which ship he has acted in the capacity of second officer. In testimony whereof I have herewith set my hand, suffixed my seal of office at the City of Canton this nineteenth day of April, 1812.
>
> (Signed) John P. Cushing"

No explanation survives for this action. It was Davis's intent to continue with the Winships and return not to Boston but to Hawaii and business with Kamehameha. With ships blockaded, how did Reynolds find passage home? Thanks to his love of poetry and to the indomitable fur trader J. J. Astor, the question is answered. The first clue is in Reynolds' handwriting on a loose sheet of paper among his letters. Admiring a ballad, and copying it for his collection, he wrote:

> "An old ballad, presented by Theodore Hunt, Esq. on a passage from Canton, in China, to New York, in America
> "3 September, 1812, at sea,
> "Lat'de 2/23 North, Long'tde 33/6 East, Ship *Hannibal*"

How did the *Hannibal* escape the blockade? According to an Astor biographer, John Upton Terrell, the *Hannibal* was waiting in Canton with a very valuable cargo, her owners and captain fearful of making the wartime trip home. Terrell says, "Astor simply bought the ship and ordered it home."

So we do not know whether the *Isabella*'s profit at Canton exceeded the wagered $120,000, or whether either Davis or Reynolds bought the other man a suit of clothes.

The exclusive contract between Kamehameha and the Lords of the Pacific was to fail. Due to the war, in their first deal with the King they were unable to deliver. Reynolds did not know of their fate until three years later, when as captain of the *Sultan,* en route to the Pacific, he received word from his owners:

"Boston, December 23, 1815
"Capt. C. Reynolds (Ship *Sultan*)
"Dear Sir:
"We embrace this opportunity, the first we have had since your departure, by the Ship *Avon,* Capt. Whittemore . . . Capt. Davis came home from Canton in the Ship *Packet* not long after you sailed. His sandalwood business and all other concerns in that quarter took a most unlucky turn and we have lost all property in that quarter. Capt. Davis will probably again visit the Pacific next year."

Davis and Reynolds met again on the coast of Chile two years later. Meantime the *Hannibal* delivered Caleb Reynolds to New York in September, 1812.

CHAPTER FOUR

"My Excellent Mary"
1812-1815

".... I am pleased with the appellation of Friend . . .
I could willingly repay you with one
of more endearing quality . . ."

Home in September, 1812, meant home to war conditions. Though shipping was idle, Reynolds remained in the employ of Boardman and Pope, but for a period of two years, neither personal records nor even poetry survive to reveal his occupation or his location.

And then a letter came from his owners dated June, 1814, addressing him in Boston as "Captain Reynolds."

He was to take command of ship *Mary Ann*, poised in Boston Harbor. But the letter advised that he delay departure "until you receive further orders from us ... we wish you to keep a close watch every night and have your after hatch always secured so that it cannot be possible for any of your people to get at the coffee, as they might pass some bags over the side into a boat."

Another year passed before Boardman and Pope sent the captain to sea.

But this was a fortunate delay.

"Beached" mariners such as Reynolds were often employed in the ship-building industry, based in the tiny inland river towns of Massachusetts.

One of these towns was Dighton on the Taunton River, where lived the fifth American generation of a large family named Williams. In 1814 the patriarch was Nathaniel, whose household included his wife Lydia, and several sons and daughters including Miss Mary.

Sent to Dighton that summer, Reynolds was introduced to the Williams family, and to Mary. They welcomed the captain cordially, and an instant sociability between Caleb Reynolds and Mary Williams led to a correspondence which continued as he was sent to various New England posts. At the end of August he wrote her from Boston:

"Boston, August 26, 1814

Miss Williams
My Good Girl
        With pleasure I avail myself of this favourable opportunity to write. I send you a little present which I brought from China, could I have known then whom it was destined for, I should have selected something of greater value . . . I do not present it with a view to bribe your memory in my favour, for I still recollect that you said you would not readily forget me . . . the voice, the accent still rests upon my ear, 'Captain I cannot believe it is true'—but I tell you, My Good Girl, that it is true. I have felt nothing like pleasure in the society of any girl since my last return to the U. States till I came to Dighton . . . and my heart still bears witness to the truth of what I have said.
        I hope, Mary, that I shall not be suspected, on your account, of writing to you, and I think I shall not, as I have taken the same liberty with

your sister . . . I venture to ask as a favour that you will take some opportunity, perhaps when you are in Providence, to drop me a line or two in the Post Office. This you can do without incurring the least suspicion. My residence is Pelham, N.H., for which I shall set out tomorrow, or Monday.

I should preserve your letter as a treasure of the richest value. I hope I shall have the opportunity of coming to Dighton again, some time this fall. The happiness which I enjoyed there I cannot enjoy in any other place, unless my Mary was present.

And believe me to be with the most honorable regard, yours most affectionately, C. Reynolds.

It is possible that the numerous Williamses, who descended from the 1630 English settler Richard Williams and his wife Frances Dighton, prided themselves on family roots and often talked of genealogy. It is genealogy which prompts the only recorded reference Reynolds ever made about his own family. Written on a loose scrap in his papers is this single clue to that mystery:

"The genealogists are at fault; I know my own parentage. My father, though array'd in rags, was a man of high pretension, and my mother was Miss Credit, a favorite daughter of the Gull family."

From Fort Washington, near Portsmouth, New Hampshire, he wrote to Mary again in October, still anxious to avoid any impropriety.

"Yesterday I received your kind and generous letter . . . I am pleased with the appellation of Friend . . . I could willingly repay you with one of more endearing quality. I am glad that you have seized the opportunity of opening a Correspondence. I hope My Dear Girl that there will be no impropriety in continuing it. If I thought there was, I certainly, for your sake, would not continue to do so. I shall venture to enclose this in a half sheet to your Brother, as I recognized his hand in the superscription of the one you had the goodness to address.

"I had it in contemplation to visit you before this, and had the call for the defence of this place not have taken place I should have been at your Father's by the middle of the present month. No trifling thing shall prevent me from visiting you this winter—your kind invitation will certainly add new energies to this first wish of my heart.

"Happy and fortunate indeed would it have been, had it pleased my owners to have continued me at Dighton. I left with regret, I shall return with delight, with the hope that some of my winter evenings will correspond in pleasure with those of the past summer—the afternoon's range over the hills of Dighton, and the evening's walk from Mr. Hathaway's will never be forgotten."

On November 27, 1814, from Pelham, New Hampshire, Reynolds explained that his late message to her was delayed by the negligence of some post masters, and delay of the mails, which "pass here once in each week," and by the press of "duties which the service required." He thanked her for sending him a little poem, then sent her one in return, cautioning her to "carefully arrange the initials of each line."

"More charming than Spring in its bloom
Are the smiles on her health-glowing face
Reflecting the tints of the Rose
Yet surpassing its brilliance and grace.
Each charm that could kindle desire,
With rapture I saw in her eyes;
In mildness and beauty they beam'd
Like the soft bluish tints of the skies.
Love moved in the steps that she trod,
Inspiring the soul with delight,
As I gazed on her elegant form,
My heart was in Love with the sight.
She appeared as she moved on the Hills
          in semblance an Angel of light."

"I have made but little proficiency in playing the Game of Back Gammon . . . The short time I was home previous to my going to Portsmouth was spent in arranging some papers which I had had on hand for several years . . . If your pleasure in imparting Precepts and Rules can equal mine in receiving them, you will be blest indeed. But I do not expect to make much progress; I am too sensible of the truth of that elegant expression of Sternes: 'When a man's thinking more of a woman than what she is saying to him, he is too apt to forget the whole.'

". . . Let me request you to accept the assurances of my most tender regard and lasting Esteem, accompanied with a thousand _____s, when I see you I will, with your permission, write it.

Yours affectionately, C. Reynolds"

By January he was again in Pelham, and it was his turn for anguish.

"My Excellent Mary—I have been waiting with the most painful anxiety to hear from you since I left Dighton . . . what my Dear Girl is the cause of this silence? Was my conduct at parting such as to merit this seeming neglect . . . with reluctance I venture to complain . . . is it possible my poor susceptible heart has deceived itself? Has it only been pursuing, with fondest hopes, pleasure which it can never realize? Why was the Phantom drest so fair, why did it smile with such fascinating grace?

"I will continue to write til I see you—the image of my Mary shall never be driven from my bosom to make room for a stranger so unwelcome as distrust!"

He left that letter unfinished and unmailed, awaiting the "once in each week" post. Unless the post brought a letter from her bidding him to Dighton, he would go to Boston and then to Canton.

Four days later in the Pelham post office he finished the letter with this postscript:

"2nd P.S. January 31, Post Office—I have just received yours of the 23rd, and I will be in Dighton I hope by the 8th or 10th of next month. My anxiety is now relieved. If the weather should moderate and the roads become passable, I shall set out the last of this week."

The roads indeed became passable. On February 19, 1815, Caleb Reynolds and Mary Eels

Williams were married in Dighton at the home of her father.

Too soon the new husband was sent away, in April to Pelham and in May to Roxbury, where he hoped Mary's brother Seth would escort her for a visit.

> "I flatter myself that I shall see you next week, however do not let it put the family to any inconvenience but come as soon as you can. Remember me kindly to all the family, yours with constancy and truth, C. Reynolds."

The orphan mariner had acquired a family.

In August he was called to be captain of the ship *Sultan*, and directed to make the familiar voyage "to the Northwest Coast of America, and thence to Canton in China."

> "Boston, Saturday evening,
> "26th August, 1815
> "My Dear Mary:
> Tonight I shall sleep on board for the first time, but intend to be on shore early enough to hand this to Mr. Dean who will pass through

Taunton & Dighton to hand you this . . . I wrote last night my wish to see you in Boston if you could make it convenient. I think we will lay here for two or three days—and should I not see you before we sail, will write by the Pilot . . . remember me with much respect to Father and Mother . . . Your Reynolds"

This first letter from the *Sultan* went off easily by the pilot of Boston Harbor. But correspondence, difficult enough during their courtship between Massachusetts towns, was now to be more difficult. Mariners sent letters when lucky enough to "speak to," or contact, another ship. Any contact for the far-flung mariners with each other or with their homes could take a year or more.

"Ship Sultan at sea
"Lat'd 29/16N—Long'de 52/26 W
"Sept. 4th, 1815
"My excellent Mary:
      "I salute you from the Great expanse of waters with health and esteem. We had a dreadfull Gale on the afternoon, and during the night, of the 31st of August, being only one day out . . . but by the blessings of a Good Providence we are yet safe . . . I am well satisfied with the officers and

crew, but pitifully we exhibited a pitiful scene, 10 or a dozen young men in the Gale crawling about the decks, drencht with rain and half buried in the billows that were frequently breaking over them but they are all well but one, whom I fear will die of sea-sickness . . .

"Yours with constant affection and love,

C. Reynolds"

"Ship Sultan, St. Catherine's
"Nov. 23rd, 1815
"My excellent wife:

". . . I have wrote you once at sea, commencing on the 4th September . . . and mentioned in that letter a severe gale of wind we had in getting out of Boston Bay—since that time we have had the weather generally good . . . The ship sails well and is otherwise one of the best vessels I ever sail'd in.

"I thought before we parted that the cares attendant on the charge committed to me would at times prevent me from thinking on you—but it is impossible, no toils or duties which I have already surmounted have been able for a moment to keep you from my mind . . . when I pray it is with the most earnest solicitude that Heaven will bless you . . . on my former voyages I felt no solicitude for home, happy in the society of my Shipmates, but it is not so now . . . even the very scenery around Dighton is constantly rising in vision before me . . ."

"O! My Mary! one tedious year must roll away, perhaps another half, before I can hear from you . . . Letters though taught to aid the wretched, travel too slow, they are dull and unimpassioned messengers at most . . . they cannot feel, they cannot kindle and glow at every emotion rising in the Soul and darting from the eyes, but they are the only means in the power of mortals . . . wait with patience and fortitude, my only Mary, for the time of our meeting. I shall never cease to love and esteem thee dearer than every other Earthly object. Your Reynolds."

How could she not wait with patience and fortitude, reading such words, even a year after their writing, and even as one year's separation stretched to two, three, and then to four.

CHAPTER FIVE

Ship *Sultan*
1815-1819

"... It is the most distressing situation that one can be placed in to encounter obstacles that cannot be surmounted by any exertions of one's own ..."

The *Sultan* was a brand new vessel, built and registered at the Charlestown, Massachusetts ship-yards August 22, 1815. The master carpenter was Josiah H. Barker. She was 274 tons, 93 feet 8 inches in length, 25 feet 10 inches in breadth, and 12 feet in depth, only slightly larger than the *Pearl* or *Isabella*. She had two decks, three masts, a square stern, no galleries, and a billet figurehead.

It is letters which tell the first half of the story of Captain Reynolds and the *Sultan*'s long maiden voyage, beginning with the owners' letter of instructions on the eve of her departure.

The Assignment

"Boston, 29 August 1815
"Capt. C. Reynolds
"Sir:

"The Ship *Sultan* being now ready to sail under your command . . . to the North West Coast of America, thence to Canton, & back to this port, our orders are, that you embrace the first fair wind and weather and proceed to sea.

"Advisable to stop at St. Catherine's for water and vegetables, taking every precaution to prevent your men deserting.

"After rounding the Horn stay clear of Spanish coast, as vessels may detain you on pretense they think your cargo for Spanish ports; go to Gallipagos and take on land tortoise and turtle, easily obtained in quantity, live a long time and prove wholesome and fresh repast for your crew and also enable you to save your fatted provisions. At Albemarle, one of this group of islands, whale's teeth may be found on the beach, buried in the sand, from whales that die in the Bay and are driven on shore. Or obtain from the whaling ships you will meet about here. Advisable to get consid-

erable quantity, they will be serviceable to you if
you visit islands in the Pacific to procure sandalwood, also provisions there. You have a box of
these teeth on board, but avoid acquiring more at
an enormous price. You may not go after the
wood, for if you succeed at the other objects of
your voyage we consider it more advantageous.
On leaving these islands proceed with dispatch to
the Russian settlements, there make sale of all
your cargo you can, taking seal skins in payment
at fair price, the only article we have been able to
obtain, as otter are held too high by them.

"Send your furs to Canton ahead, or get a
storage place from Baranof before going hunting.
After making sales, endeavor immediately before
other vessels fall in there to procure on contract
Kodiak Hunters and Canoes and proceed after
otter skins, sending any off to Perkins at Canton.
Also land parties for sealing, (and we suggest arrange some sort of reward for the man commanding the party) returning at stated times to take off
their collections. We do not confine you to particular places but give you full liberty to go where
you please for seals, using your own crew, and if
in want of more men they can always be obtained
by a run to Sandwich islands, where you may also
want to go for provisions. If you receive specie
for your cargo, it will procure sandalwood at the
Sandwich Islands en route to Canton. Should you
be disappointed in the sealing and or the canoes,
turn your attention to a load of Sandalwood for

China, but we consider the others more important.

"If you go for wood, the whales teeth are now said to be the best article, especially at Marquesas where nothing else will buy wood. You have however on board such articles of trade which should answer, and a blacksmith prepared to furnish anything necessary in iron.

"Getting wood at Marquesas will take much time, difficulties, cannot approach in four or five leagues, coral reefs, and wood must be brought off through a considerable sea by small parcels in your Boats, making one trip each per day. Also be constantly on guard against natives, some islands very savage.

"We have found profitable hunting on Coast of California, barter trade for otters, or get specie for your trade. This must approach with great caution, not expose to capture ... more risk than formerly, do not trust information from shore; do not anchor without man at mast head, do not lay long in any place, shift often, to avoid arrest. Also, be vigilant against Kodiak hunters embezzling your skins, it has been the case.

"Your ship is new and well fitted, and crew good, so if you like, go to Canton and return to the Pacific with sufficient inducement rather than return home.

"For your services we agree to allow you twenty dollars wages per month, and seven per cent of the net proceeds of all property received as earnings of the voyage. No trade allowed except for owners' account.

"Whiteness of the whales teeth much superior to elephant, and remember the large ones would sell in Canton. Those we purchase here come at extravagant price. Some such teeth were sent to Sandwich for provisions, and if natives have not cut them up you can buy them for a trifle.

"Relying on you for exertion in our interest, and trusting your prudence and good judgment, wishing you health and prosperity, we remain,

"Your Friends, Boardman and Pope."

The Bill of Lading

August 23, 1815—Shipped in good order and well conditioned by Boardman and Pope, Native Citizens of the United States of America, residing in Boston, for their absolute account and risk in and upon the Ship called Sultan whereof is Master, for this present voyage, Caleb Reynolds, now in the Harbour of Boston and bound for the North West Coast of America and Canton.

Viz. Five Cases Cotton Velvets – One Case Cotton Hose – Four Cases Cotton Shirtings – One hhd loaf sugar – Fifty sides Leather – Seventy barrels tar – Five bbls turpentine – Ten bbls Pitch – Ten bbls Rozin – Five bbls Bright Varnish – Two hhds Hams – One Cask Linseed Oil – Twenty three Cannisters boiled

linseed Oil – Forty grindstones – Two Kegs flints –
Fifteen hhds and fifty barrels Meal – Seventy hhds,
one half pipe & two bbls Rice – Fifty one kegs Powder – One thousand & ten bars round Iron – Four
hundred seventy nine bars flat iron – Two boxes bul-
lets – Two hhds Paints – One hundred and fifty bbls
Flour – Five bags Coffee – thirty bbls Vinegar – Five
bbls Glauber salts – Two kegs Axes – Two Kegs
Hatchets – Three hhds and three kegs Butter – Six
bags and two bundles Pepper – Four half bbls & three
half pieces Irish Beef – Thirty bbls Pork – Fifty seven
bbls Beef – One Iron Sugar Boiler – Seventeen Casks
Nails – Two kegs spikes – Two boxes cont' Seven jugs
Oil – Nine cascs Glass Ware – Three Crates Bottles –
Seventeen Crates Crokery – Twenty Five Boxers
Soap – Two Arm Chests cont + Musket Balls, Nails,
Muskets, Cutlasses, Boarding Hatchets &ce – One
hundred twenty one bbls & seventy three hhds Bread
– Seventy eight hhds , five bbls Molasses – Seventy
two hhds One half pipe, two gl casks & two Kegs
Rum – Two bundles Iron Hoops – One Box Knives
– Nineteen boxes brown & one Box White Sugar –
One bbl salmon – Two Chests Tea – Three hhds To-
bacco – Ten Cases Olive Oil – Five Casks Hollow
Iron Ware – Ten Casks Raisins – Five half pipes Red
Wine – Five gl Casks Malaga Wine – Six boxes Fish –
One Cask Boots & Shoes – One Keg Shott – Two
Casks hard Ware – four Boxes Window Glass – Two
Boxes Cooking Glasses – Two bundles Frying Pans –
four doz. Iron Wire – Two hhds glass – One bundle
Butchers Steels – One Box Hats – One Keg Colouring
– Four brls Tin Ware – One Bbl Mustard – Five bars
steel – ten bbls corn – Nine and three qt Cords Wood

– Three bbls and two bags Beans – One bag Cocoa –
Three boxes chocolate – One box Candles – Four
Cheeses – Six doz Ax halves – six doz Hatchet helves
– Twenty pieces Russia Duck – Twenty pc. Ravens
Duck – Six doz. W.O. Clubs – One box cont+
whales teeth. –

Total $33,994

"... *being marked and numbered as in the
margin, and are to be delivered, in like good order
and well conditioned, at the aforesaid Port of North
West Coast & Canton (the danger of the Seas only excepted) unto the said Master or to his assigns, he or
they paying Freight for the said Goods—nothing—the
whole being owners property—without Primage and
Average. In Witness Thereof, the Master of the said
Ship hath affirmed to five Bills of Lading of this
Tenor and Date: one being accomplished, the other
four to stand void. Dated in BOSTON Aug 23 1815.*

Caleb Reynolds
Countersigned, Boardman and Pope."

Round the Horn

Reynolds did not tell Mary that in Brazil several men deserted the ship. Thus even before pass-
ing "the dreaded Horn" the *Sultan* encountered
weather more difficult than the Horn's threat, and

only three months out of Boston she suffered the
desertion of some crew. But her passage around the
Horn proved to be smooth.

"Ship Sultan, Gallapagos Islands
"Feb. 26, 1816
"My Excellent Mary—My Wife—My Friend
"I have the opportunity to write via a ship
bound for Chile . . . there is now a line of Post
across the Continent, and couriers frequently pass-
ing. I have no doubt but this will reach you sooner
than any other way by which I could hereafter
write.
"I had the shortest, and the most comfortable
passage round Cape Horn that I ever knew, without the least accident whatever, and arrived in the
Pacific all in good health. But as yet I can say
nothing on the success of the voyage, not having
reacht the first Port of our destination, for which
I will sail tomorrow and expect by the middle of
April to be there . . . I have stood the fatigue of the
voyage thus far much better than I could have expected after being on shore so long . . .
"Mary, I have not forgot that this Month is
February, I am constantly thinking on you . . .
your society would be of more value to me than
all the wealth of Asia, and should it please the Al-

mighty to grant me safe return, I will never leave
you unless driven by the imperious hand of Neces-
sity. I hope the sacrifice you have made will meet
with its due reward, and that Heaven will bless my
labours for your sake . . .

Your Reynolds"

It was mid April, 1816, when the *Sultan*
reached the "first Port of our destination,"
Norfolk Sound. Times had changed in Sitka
since his voyages with the *Pearl* in 1804 and the
Isabella in 1810. Competition between Americans supplying the Russian settlement had
increased, and he was disappointed in offering
his cargo there.

Departing Sitka, he sailed south along the
California coast as far as San Luis Obispo, then
back to Sitka in October. Here at last he
received a letter from Mary!

"Norfolk Sound, 20 Oct. 1816
"My dear Mary
   ". . . Your kind and welcome letter has given
me much pleasure . . . to read what your heart had
dictated and your hand had written was a favor
that I did but little expect this side of Canton . . .

Often when I have been reflecting on the disappointments that have attended the first part of the voyage, I have been almost ready to despair of success; till one thought alone has put the whole to flight—that I was the husband of Mary Williams whose virtues and goodness demanded every exertion that my feeble powers were capable of."

He sent her mother a snuff box given him by Governor Baranov and said he had instructed his friend Captain McNeil to procure her some money in Canton and to buy her "an umbrella of the neatest fashion," asking her not to draw upon her father "although the voyage may yet eventuate in such a manner as to render such assistance absolutely necessary."

His difficulties along the Pacific coast are revealed by subsequent letters from Boardman and Pope:

"Boston Dec. 23 1815
"Captain C. Reynolds
    "Dear Sir
    "We embrace this opportunity . . . to forward you a Nautical Almanac for 1817, and to say that we hope you arrived out safe, and are

prosecuting a profitable business, although we were a little apprehensive that you might have experienced some accident in the violent gale which took place two days after you sailed, until some vessels have been heard from which sailed at the same time.

"Recommend you take hair seals when you can, without neglecting your other objects . . . but get canoes if you can and prosecute that business . . . to any advantage, for we consider you will raise capital faster that way than any other.

"The almanac we sent you is the American edition—compare it with Whittemore's English edition.

"You might take a number of Sandwich islanders with a white man at their head for the purpose of taking hair seal—but recollect, must keep your concerns distinct from any other vessel, even the *Orina* or *Isabella*.

"Your friends, Boardman and Pope"

"Boston Aug. 5th 1816
"Capt. C. Reynolds, Sir:

"We were very glad to receive a letter from you at St. Catherine's, and to hear of your safe arrival there [Nov. 1815] in consequence of the very violent gale we experienced the day after your sailing . . . We regret to learn that you lost some of your men in Brazil by desertion.

"We send this by Capt. Suter in the Ship *Mentor*. Capt. Davis will sail in November for Norfolk Sound in a ship of ours called *Eagle*. If you have opportunity, it may be well to let Gov. Baranof know it.

"If you attempt to save the Hair Seal with a view of sending the skins to America, they should be thrown into a strong pickle, and then stretched out fair with pegs until they are dried. If pickled and not stretched, they swell up as thick as one's finger and thus occupy much room . . . Business is very dull, which is not confined to the United States but extends all over the Commercial World, and is the consequence of an universal peace after an European War of twenty thrice years."

"Boston Dec. 3, 1816
"Capt. C. Reynolds, Sir,
    "We forward to you by Captain Davis, the *Eagle*, our letter of October 18 and refer you to him for the state of the times with us. Rec'd yours of February last at Gallipagos . . . urge you con-

tract for canoes, the price of California otter being 27 dollars last May."

"Boston Oct. 6, 1817 Via *Volunteer*

". . . Since we last wrote you on the 18th Oct. 1816, we have received your letters of 6th May and 18 Oct. 1816 . . . we regret the unfavorable market at Norfolk Sound . . . we find that you had been at the Columbia River, regret that you had been cheated in your dollars received for goods, which prove to have been many of base silver—you intended trying again to get canoes, and also in selling such parts of your cargo at Norfolk Sound as were perishable. If not employed with canoes, we hope you have met with some success in sealing and obtaining Sandal Wood, such as to enable you to go to Canton, where if you have not funds enough of your own earnings to load you, you must fill up with freight for home under the direction of Mr. Cushing. By our last advices from the Marquesas, nothing but Muskets would procure Sandal Wood."

When Reynolds wrote to Perkins & Company in Canton, they replied:

"Canton, January 22, 1817

"... sea otter are now 20 dollars a pair and no doubt will be preferred next season to other furs. We have paid Capt. McNeil agreeable to your request 100 dollars to purchase articles for your family, which he forwarded by Capt. N. Winship who left here in December for America. The price of sandalwood is improving here, now worth 14 dollars ... Russian bills drawn on St. Petersburg are said to be good for nothing—we mention this that you might be on your guard.

"With esteem, your obe' servants,

"Perkins & Co."

At the Sandwich Islands

The captain was scrambling. His efforts through 1816 were spent in any and all directions suggested by the owners, and for his own interest as well he tried them all: hiring canoes for otter, sealing, and seeking sandalwood.

Only his correspondence told the tale, until March 10, 1817, when entries begin in his captain's log. These pages, written from this date through his homecoming September 3, 1819, make plain the work involved in management and navigation of the ship and particularly the laborious process of gathering sandalwood in the Sandwich Islands and in the Marquesas. They also record the *Sultan*'s encounters with the revolutionaries in Chile, the H.M.S. *Bounty* mutineers at Pitcairn, and some mutineers of her own.

The log entries begin at Cabo San Lucas. He has roamed the Pacific coast once more, south from Sitka in October 1816, visiting the Columbia River, finally reaching Mexico. Leaving the Baja coast in March, he headed for the Sandwich Islands, arriving at the island of Oahu, April 21.

"Remarks 22 April, 1817—

". . . at 3:30 pm, wind off Diamond Hill. Pilot came on board while Ship was not yet to windward of the Anchoring place. Mr. Hairbottle, the Pilot, came on Board to pilot us to the anchoring place. Captain Blanchard, *Bordeaux Packett*, direct from Boston, called on Board but brought no letters."

Reynolds had become acquainted with various people in the Sandwich Islands when aboard the

Pearl in 1806. They included Mr. Pitt, or Trymokoo, the island trader, from whom he now bought hogs and taro. He did not intend to enter the Honolulu harbor, which required the pilot to navigate the bar and also required an anchoring charge. But he went ashore with Captain Lewis, of the *Panther*, while waiting for his watering party.

> "Remarks 25 April, 1817—
>
> ". . . At evening the Boat returned with the last load of water, so I had no inducement to stop except business with Captain Lewis. The principal object I had in coming here was to take a small Gang of Sealers, with Mr. Navarra at their head, who was to have them engaged and ready on my arrival here—which I expected would have been in February or March—however I found that he had not engaged any, and that he appeared rather indifferent about the business. To wait longer would only prove an unprofitable waste of time & I therefore determined to run up to Owyhee & there endeavor to get what few people I might want. Mr. Jones found Charles Gibson conveying rum from the storeroom in a bladder, for which I will punish him in the morning."

When Navarra came up with terms, they were such that Reynolds "could not accede to" and he made way for the island of Hawaii to find the King.

The passage from Oahu to Hawaii gave heavy, choppy seas and caused the ship to labor considerably, "the sea not subsiding made the Ship very uneasy and split several light sails."

"Remarks 30 April, 1817—
". . . Finally anchored at Tocaigh [Kawaihae, on Hawaii's west coast] where we found the *Enterprise*, Capt. Ebbets, of New York and *Zephyr* of Providence, Capt. Brintnall. Brintnall had the politeness to come off in his Boat and conduct us to the proper anchorage. Bought of Capt. Ebbets some indifferent muskets and some Slop clothes, paid in goods."

"Remarks 1 May, 1817—
". . . The King came on board with many of his retinue, and I made some arrangements for trade. I shipped 5 of the islanders in order to strengthen my crew . . . 4 May—landed the last of the bulky articles the King had purchased."

He now wrote Mary both good and bad news.

". . . I have just sold a part of the outward bound cargo to the King of these islands, the celebrated Tamehameha . . . the prospects of making a good voyage still remain gloomy. I shall leave here tomorrow for the Marquesas and if I succeed in the business I am going on, I shall in all probability be in Canton by the end of the year, and if the prospect is no better than at present, I shall return home . . . I have received a letter from Canton, reassuring me about my arrangements for you with Capt. McNeil and N. Winship . . . should I not return this year, I will send you more money that you may not be altogether depended on your good Father."

Many a fur trader, provisioning at the Sandwich Islands en route to Canton, added sandalwood to his cargo. Even the famous cargo of John Suter in 1810, with over 6,000 otter pelts, had been augmented with sandalwood from Hawaii. This wood, plentiful in Hawaii and in the scattered Marquesas Islands, became the coveted item to be offered in Canton. By 1817, sea otters were so diminished that their trade was effectively over, and for a decade had been gradually replaced by sandalwood.

King Kamehameha controlled the sandal-wood industry. The King continued to welcome all traders, but he alone made all the deals. The wood was cut to the specified "size of a ship's hold" lengths, measured in a trench dug to the proper size. Men, women and children carried the wood from the forests down the mountain-sides to their waiting canoes. But the natives could not ferry the wood to the ships anchored off the shore until the King approved.

A trader needed to catch up with the King as he and his retinue moved from port to port. While Reynolds pursued the roving King for wood, he also coped with a rebellious crew. His armorer, after drinking, used "insolent and abu-sive" language and was ordered below. Continu-ing his provoking behavior he was put in irons.

"Remarks 4 May, 1817—
"... one of the natives who lived in the same part of the ship ... reported the Armourer had pistols ... I overhauled him and found in his bosom a loaded pistol and a large knife and in the waistband of his trousers another loaded pistol ...

Captain Brintnall agreed the armourer meant mutiny and murder and he was put in confinement."

By May 10 they reached the King to get the promised wood plus fifteen hogs.

". . . The hogs I got, but not the wood—it will be ready <u>October next!!</u>"

The King's wood delivery was indeed delayed, and well beyond "October next." Reynolds spent the next four months in the Marquesas seeking sandalwood. Then, in that "October next," instead of returning to the Sandwich Islands, or much less going on to Canton, he tried his luck at Massafuero for seal and proceeded to Chile where he hoped to trade his outbound cargo and purchase copper. He reached Valparaiso only to be detained by the revolutionaries—and to suffer more desertions.

There would be another May on the calendar and another two months at the Marquesas before he could return to the Sandwich Islands in July, 1818.

At the Marquesas Islands
May – September, 1817

"Remarks 16 May, 1817—
". . . ship under all sail leaving Owyhee, with
light wind and clear weather, the sea smooth with
a moderate swell from the southeast, remarkably
fine and pleasant, at 11 hours 32 AM the Long'de
by 3 sets of the Distances of Moon with the Sun
was 150/21W. Lat'de by Obsn. 23/53N."

The islands the *Sultan* was approaching rise
from the sea abruptly, like mammoth rocks, with
the ocean pounding against cliffs and rocky
shores. A few bays which could afford closer
approaches were equally difficult, with swells
that often repulsed an approaching ship. The
trading ship could only tack and tack again to
find a mooring as near the shore as possible, then
send her boats in to the shores. Behind the for-
bidding coastlines, the interiors of the islands
were fertile, producing vegetables and wild
hogs—and sandalwood.

Boardman and Pope had painted a true picture of what was ahead in the Marquesas. The
trips from island to island were laborious, with

wind, rain, hard currents, and frequent squalls.
But Reynolds found cordiality rather than hostil-
ity with most native leaders. He referred to "my
new friend Mannahaw, the young chief" and to
many visitors. And there were scenes of beauty.
Occasionally on a calm evening, native fishermen
would fill a bay with lighted torches to lure fish
to shore or surface, making a beautiful illumina-
tion.

"Remarks 4 June, 1817—
    "Began with fresh breezes & cloudy weather.
At noon the sun broke through the clouds & gave
an opportunity to observe his attitude, which gave
the Lat'de 15/43 North.

"Remarks 14 June, 1817—
    ". . . This day one of the Sows which I had
bought of the King Tamaahmaah & which proved
to be forward with pig produced a litter of 5 pigs,
making with the 7 which our old Ship Sow had
just produced, twelve young, all likely to do well."

"Remarks 21 June, 1817—
    ". . . we were now passing through a space of
navigation but little traversed, & in the neighbor-
hood of a Group of islands said to have been discovered by the Spaniards a few years past—I there-

fore charged the officers to cause a faithful lookout to be kept."

"Remarks 26 June, 1817—
    ". . . The Island of Magdalena came in sight, and we hove to for some canoes that came from shore, about a mile distant. They informed us, as near as we understood them, that there were plenty of Hogs on other parts of the Island. They brought off some breadfruit, potatoes and one small hog. We hove to again for more native canoes, in one of which were two women who brought 2 hogs to sell, but as they wanted nothing but Beads for them I could not buy, having none of that article . . . I was led to believe I could get hogs by waiting til morning, but no success. Next day tacked back and forth for canoes that might come, bought two small hogs. Disappointed in my expectations of obtaining hogs here I stood off to the NW for St. Christiana, where we held our station til daylight that we might run close in and barter with natives for hogs and fruit, but weather prevented. Constant lightning from all parts of the heavens, attended with heavy squalls and showers of rain.
    ". . . When weather became clear bore away for Massachusetts Bay where we had the good fortune to run up the Bay to more than half its depth,

when the flow took us so much ahead we were obliged to drop anchor in 15 fathoms water, afterward warpt up into 9 fathoms & then let go the Stream and steadied the ship with the Pidge.

"Soon after, Charles Payson of Boston came on board, he had lately left the Brig *Panther*, Capt. Lewis. He told us that Typee natives had killed and eaten the Cooper who deserted *Panther*, and others had killed an Irishman."

"Remarks 30 June, 1817—

". . . visited by Mannahaw, the King's grandson, a man of much popularity and distinction. His conduct was orderly, decent and unassuming. He took dinner with us and remained onboard overnight. At 8 AM saw a Ship which proved to be the *Resource* of New York, Captain Sole, direct from that place.

"Next day went ashore with Capt. Sole to make a formal visit to the King or principal Chief who came off to the Ship and took dinner with us on *Sultan*. I made him a present of a small whalestooth. Mannahaw remained the afternoon with one of the principal warriors.

"Exchanged with Capt. Sole 55 lbs. flat Bar Iron for the same weight of nail rods . . . Capt. Sole, my new friend Mannahaw and I went into the country a short distance to search for some wood that would answer for Gunstocking should we want it, without finding any."

"Remarks 4 July, 1817—

". . . This day being the Anniversary of our National Independence I caused all duty to be suspended but such was absolutely necessary & in the morning sat all colours and fired a Gun . . . and gave the Ships company as good a dinner as my situation would admit of—with a moderate allowance of Grog."

"Remarks 7 July, 1817—

". . . Sent Mr. Newell off for Lewis Bay with Thomas Austin, the Malay who had engaged to Trade and Interpret for me. They returned with 1259 lbs of wood which they could obtain for a Musket"

"Remarks 22 July, 1817—

"Began with steady fresh breezes— endeavoring to work into the bay, having been twice drifted out & obliged to make sail—at 3 PM we rounded the Point a third time & stretcht over to the Starboard shore and tackt & while the Ship was in stays, took in all the sail, having plenty of hands from the other vessels—during the night calm & quiet—part of forenoon with Captain

Campbell, on *Daphne* bartering with him for sandalwood."

"Remarks 25 July, 1817—
    "... seeing the *King George,* Captain Walker,
heave in sight off the Harbour . . . stopt til she
should get along side, expecting Capt. Walker intended to purchase some of my Rum . . . He
brought with him an Irishman, James Sullivan,
who had been two years among the islands & who
wished to leave them in some Ship that might be
bound toward the Sandwich Islands or China—&
giving the man a good Character I concluded to
take him onboard for his passage—& in case he
rendered any particular & profitable services to
make him some pecuniary satisfaction."

Sullivan indeed proved helpful more than
once in confrontations with natives over wood
and discipline of the hired natives. At Dominica
the King sent a messenger to say the Valley
wished to make a gift and asked for the *Sultan*'s
boat to bring them off the beach. Suspecting
some treachery the captain deemed it imprudent
to send any white person, so he sent two
"kanackers" to bring aboard the King, who in-

formed him he intended to fight the enemy tomorrow and asked for help.

"Remarks 6 August, 1817
"...I replied that I came to buy sandalwood,
not to fight, but that if their Enemy came in to
destroy their village that I would drive them off
with our Cannon; with which assurance he was
satisfied, and requested the Boat might go in and
bring off the Present they intended me—it con-
sisted of 3 Boat loads of Bread, Coconuts, Bananas,
with 13 small Hogs. With the last load came off
his wife & a sister—to each of the women I gave 2
yds of cotton cloth & to the King 20 Musket Cartridges."

"Remarks 10 September, 1817—
"...At 1 PM Mr. Newell returned with the
Pinnace to the small bay . . . at 6 they returned
well loaded with hogs & a few trifling articles. Set
out for Resolution Bay—at daylight saw a ship we
took for the *Resource* but concluded the stranger
was the *Flying Fish* of Boston, Captain Fitch,
which proved to be the case."

Remarks 11 September, 1817—
"...At 1 PM spoke to the stranger and at
1/2 past 2 Captain Fitch and Mr. Garrah a Spanish
gentleman came onboard & remained with us until sunset . . . in order to oblige Captain Fitch who

was a stranger I consented that Sullivan should go
onboard with him and remain about 10 days. We
then made sail for Nooehewah, where we found
Captain Sole, he had arrived only the day before."

The *Sultan* had sailed six weeks from the
Sandwich Islands to reach the Marquesas, and
there they worked three months. About thirty-
five "lots" of wood were recorded in this time, as
large as 2,819 pounds or as small as 300 pounds,
and were described as "fine" or "successful" or "of
indifferent, tolerable, poor quality" or "too
dirty." Indeed the crew needed to clean or remove "sap" from most of the wood bought any-
where before offering it at Canton. While most
often muskets would buy sandalwood here, one
day Reynolds bought 14 hogs with 7 whalesteeth.
In one visit with the young Chief Mannahaw, the
latter requested he and Reynolds exchange
names, a custom expressing special friendship.

The Marquesas log ends with "Now ready to
go on a sailing voyage toward Cape Horn." Cape
Horn lay in the direction they pursued, but they
were heading for Chile.

Pitcairn Island

October 16 – 20, 1817

On the first of October, 1817, the *Sultan* set out for Massafuero off the Chilean coast. This was the "October next" when sandalwood was promised by King Kamehameha, but the *Sultan* was bound elsewhere. En route to Massafuero he came upon the tiny island of Pitcairn and the last survivor of the H.M.S. *Bounty* mutiny. The log tells the story.

"Remarks 1 October 1817—
". . . I have taken from the Marquesas at their own request, three persons, one a native of Tahiti, one a boy, a native of New Zealand, and the other a native of Noochiwa, a young man whom I could not without violence oblige to leave the ship."

"Remarks 2 October 1817—
". . . Split the main Top Galt sail from head to foot, it was much worne having been constantly in use since we left Boston. No obsn. Lat'de by acct. 10/28 South."

"Remarks 4 October 1817—
". . . Cloudy, squally, split the Jib, employed mending it & cleaning remainder of sandalwood."

"Remarks 7 October 1817—

". . . Long'de by 3 sets of distances of Sun & Moon at 139/14 West—Employed repairing sails— at 6 AM saw land bearing SE/E about 5 leagues, of no great height. As no island is marked on my Charts within less than one degree of Lat'de, we have taken it for a new discovery and as recompense for the vigilance of the man who first saw it, I have called it Turner's Island. The situation of Turner's Island, according to our Obsn is Lat'de 17/18 South, Long'de 138/30 West."

"Remarks 8 October 1817—

". . . Sent the Whale Boat in shore with Mr. Newell, with a view to purchase Hogs and fruit if he found the inhabitants friendly inclined, but on reaching shore he found them so averse to any communication that he retired very soon. Harry the Sandwich Islander and Dick the Tahitian could neither of them understand the language. They were all armed with large spears and slings. They were much darker than the natives of Sandwich but not tatooed like those of the Marquesas. Those assembled on the beach were to the number of nearly 200. At 4 PM the Boat returned—at 7 gentle breezes sprung up from the No. & East'd &

increased until midnight to which we carried all sail with providence, keeping a constant lookout."

The *Sultan* proceeded south, the crew making the new top gallant sail and cleaning sandalwood, the carpenter making a new Whale Boat. The armorer was on sick list, and George Rodgers was on duty with Sumner, Cassel, Loring and Shattuck and two of the "Kanackers," or natives.

"Remarks 16 October 1817—
"...At 2 hours 28 PM the Long'tde by three sets of distances of the Moon with the Sun was 130/56 West. At 6 PM squally with rain, took in all the light sail—at 8 sat the Jib & Spaner, let one reef out of Main Top Sail & sat the Main Top Galt. At 2 PM, having gained the Lat'de assigned to Pitcairn's Island according to Capt. Staines of the British Frigate *Briton*, and from our Lunar Obsn. not more than 45 or 50 miles to the West'd of it, we shortened sail and laid the Ship's head to the SW until daylight. At 2 PM saw Pitcairn's Island 6 or 7 leagues distant, and at 5 PM, being opposite the village on the SW part of the island and the wind being moderate, sent the Whale Boat in shore. She returned about sunset, bringing off four of the inhabitants of the place—they were the immediate descendants of the Mutineers of the

Bounty. They spoke very good English and were well instructed in morals and religion. They expressed great pleasure in seeing us and made offers of an abundant supply of refreshments, which they said would be ready early in the morning, as most of their people had gone to collect them. As it was getting late, I invited them to spend the night on board, and that the Boat should go in early in the morning. The evening proved cloudy, and the wind began to increase."

Boardman and Pope had told Reynolds, "We believe but few inhabitants at Pitcairn, those descended from some of the Bounty's Crew who fled there with some Indian women."

Twenty-eight years had now passed since the famous mutiny of Fletcher Christian and others who set their Captain William Bligh adrift, stole H.M.S. *Bounty*, and disappeared for eighteen years. Then in 1808 an American sealing ship, the *Topaz*, Captain Matthew Folger, came upon the island and the captain was startled to see smoke. He knew the island from his chart, but believed it uninhabited and never yet visited by a white man. Pitcairn Island had been charted by the explorer Carteret, H.M.S. *Swallow*, in 1767.

It is said that Fletcher Christian remembered those charts when he sought refuge in 1790.

Captain Folger had found the hidden colony. He was their first contact with the outside world since settling on Pitcairn. The islanders told him they had seen one ship in 1795, but hid in the bush in alarm. Folger and the *Topaz* were welcomed, and the captain recorded it in his log and sent a report to Australia, but little notice was taken of it. Folger reported speaking with Alexander Smith, the elderly leader, who was the last surviving mutineer and was now alone with the native wives, teaching the second generation.

It is not likely that the *Sultan* stopped with sandalwood in mind, rather for refreshment, even though this island, being mostly mountainous rock, rose abruptly from the sea and afforded only one landing place safe from treacherous rocks. In 1814 two British ships, H.M.S. *Briton*, Captain Staines, and H.M.S. *Tagus*, Captain Pipon, came upon the island while at war with America and searching for Captain David Porter of the U.S.S. *Essex*. Folger's "Alexander Smith" now called himself "John Adams," after the former American president, hoping to cover his identity. Staines and Pipon told stories similar to Folger's but for this new name, which much interested the world. Still the British did not pursue Adams.

Reynolds hosted the Pitcairners aboard *Sultan*, while the log described difficult weather lasting two days, which prevented the return of their boats.

> "Remarks 19 October, 1817—
> "Began with light winds and clear weather. The winds generally from the N.W. At 3 PM the whale boat returned, bringing off Mr. John Adams, the only surviving person of the Bounty's crew who came to this Island on her. The boat also brought off several goats, pigs and fowles. Adams made us an offer of a liberal supply of hogs, vegetables and every refreshment the island afforded. The boats made three trips to the shore and as the surf was high we found it dangerous to attempt doing anything in the night . . . the inhabitants agreeing to bring down the yams and other articles during the night in case we would remain

until daylight which I consented to do . . . at daylight the two Boats were sent in, making two trips each. We got off some of the copper of the *Bounty*. Adams also gave me the Spying Glass that belonged to the Master of the Ship *Bounty*. For the supply of Provisions I gave them 2 axes, 2 Hatchets, and 2 Iron Plate Handsaws with a few other trifling articles. Adams remained with us until our departure. The inhabitants were hospitable and friendly to an extreme degree."

"Remarks 20th October 1817—
    "Began with light winds from the North with particularly clear weather inclining to haze. At 3 PM the last Boat returned and having got on board an abundant supply of hogs, goats and Yams, we parted with the friendly people, having let them have the small stern Boat, that was almost useless to the ship, to go ashore in."

At sea two days later one of the Pitcairn goats brought forth two kids, and the armorer was occupied making nails from the *Bounty* copper. The *Sultan* departed for points east, and when they reached Massafuero, Reynolds and Mr. Newell set off for the shore.

"Remarks 15th November 1817—

". . . the crew prepared with clubs and knives to begin killing and skinning Seal which I had no doubt but we should find, but to my great disappointment after searching most of the place where they formerly had been taken, found only 3 on the rocks, one of which we killed.

"Proceeding toward Chile, all hands employed parcelling out the small Bower and Stream cables from both of which we were obliged to cut several fathoms, having got injured at Marquesas, but I wanted them in good order as possible in case it should become absolutely necessary to anchor for the Safety of the Ship while on the Coast. 31/40S— 74/51 West."

It was necessary, as it turned out, to anchor on the Coast of Chile, where the *Sultan* encountered deep trouble with the authorities.

Chile
November 1817 – April 1818

In spite of presenting letters of introduction for trading in Santiago and Guasco, Reynolds found little success in selling his out-bound cargo on the coast of Chile. While anchored at Coquimbo he received letters from colleague Captain Henry Dorr of the Boston ship *Ida*, confirming that the markets in Chile were glutted. Dorr wrote that the Chilean government, now in revolt against Spain, and hoping to prevent Spanish privateering, was detaining all ships.

". . . Privateering here is so fashionable that all my crew have absconded and I remain in the *Ida* unable to get a single seaman to navigate my Ship . . . I came last from Gibraltar to get a cargo of copper for China, and I have a cargo at Coquimbo . . . keep a good watch, as there is a fleet expected at these ports from Lima with troops and if taken we will make good prizes . . . The *Canton* of Providence was taken off Conception lately, and *Beaver* of New York from this harbour . . . I understand Coquimbo is not in a state of defense.

"I am sorry for the unpropitious prospect of your voyage . . . I have the same . . . Chile fears invasion, I think . . . Tell me if you have Master Boardman still with you and how he performs. Thank you for your offer of men but they would just run away . . . I have only 2 plus myself, so no prospect of leaving. The reports from home say commerce is ruinous."

On January 29 Reynolds wrote Mary, "Chile, but not Peru, is in the hands of the patriots—Chile's troubles are as much with Peruvian royalist neighbors as with Spain." He told her that he had expected to have finished his trade in Chile by now and be on his way to Canton. "Alas, not this year! So I must endeavor to add something more to the voyage until the return of the next season."

The *Sultan* was one of many ships detained by the blockade, but Reynolds like Dorr suffered double outrage. Just as he gained clearance to depart in early February, several of his men deserted to a privateer in Coquimbo harbor. But it was a Chilean, not a Spanish ship to which they ran away. Incensed by the Chilean action, he wrote to the authorities:

"Saturday, 7th Febr. 1818—Coquimbo
   "Caleb Reynolds, Master of the Ship or Vessel called the *Sultan* of Boston, of the size of two hundred and seventy four tons or thereabouts, mounting eight guns and navigated by one Master, three Mates, one Carpenter, one Armourer and nineteen seamen, cook and steward included, and

laden with sundry articles of merchandise consisting of Rice, Rum, Sugar, Tar, Flour, Iron, Cotton Goods, etc. etc., as may be seen by Invoice—Sailed from Boston on a trading voyage to the Northwest Coast of America and Canton, during the prosecution of which the original ship's company had been reduced by one Mate and seven seamen, which number had been replaced by persons, natives of the Marquesas and Sandwich Islands; and that after leaving the Marquesas or Washington Islands arrived at the Fort of Coquimbo within the jurisdiction of the supreme Government of Chile, on the 19th day of November, 1817, but fearing damages, enters his protest accordingly:

"After having disposed of a considerable part of my cargo and receiving copper in payment for the same at the Port of Coquimbo, intended with fifty tons of sandalwood already on board for the China Market, and having obtained a regular clearance from the Collector of the Customs as related to duties payable on Goods that had been sold in the district, and was only waiting in Port to adjust my accounts with my Consignee, Don Francisco Bascunan Calle, when on the 6th day of the present month, February, the same day that I had obtained my clearance at 2 o'clock P.M. the private armed Brig *Mercedas de la Fortuna* commanded by a Capt. James Hardy or Harley, and bearing the Flag of the Government of Chile, entered the Port of Coquimbo and came to anchor within a short distance of the vessels then Laying there and within point-blank shot of the guns of the Battery.

"And that on the 7th of the present month, at 5 o'clock P.M. six of my seamen, namely: Silas Turner, Charles Sumner, Jesse Downes, John M. Loring, Joseph Cassell and George Rodgers—in the momentary absence of the officer of the Deck who was attending to some duty below, took the boat, the only one then along side the Ship, and proceeded with the greatest precipitation to the aforesaid private armed Brig, where they were received on board and the boat left adrift . . ."

After sending this formal protest to the Governor he made a trip with the Commandant and Mr. Newell to board the privateer, where they were refused both the men and the right to search for them. The men didn't want to be reclaimed.

Stranded without manpower, he hoped for military aid, and wrote to the American warship *Ontario*, based in Santiago. Saying they were unable to come to Coquimbo, the *Ontario* advised that all Spanish officers were currently ordered to seize all ships which tried to enter or leave the harbor.

Reynolds then protested in a letter to Governor Pecavarren that the *Fortuna* captain, a Chilean privateer, was more dangerous than the Spanish. The Governor disclaimed any responsibility for individual deserters, and when Reynolds suggested their government be liable for damages, the Governor called it a "scandalous idea."

With no recourse visible or help forthcoming, Reynolds seriously considered selling or abandoning the ship, but his friend Dorr advised against it, saying the Chilean government was too poor to buy any ship, and would barter instead with broken down, stolen ships. The same advice came from his friend Captain Solomon Townsend, stranded in Santiago.

On February 21 he sent Mary a brief account of this delay, and told her that among the deserters were Charles Sumner and "young Downes."

"... I always intended to have placed young Downes and Sumner, before the close of the voyage, in positions which would give them prominence, but they did not hesitate to do me almost irreparable injury ... I have but four white men onboard excepting the two officers, and unless the *Ontario* can supply me with six or seven seamen, I will not be able to prosecute the voyage as intended ... impossible to arrive Canton this season, and . . . obliged to prolong the voyage another year ... I am sorry to relate this, but ... you should know it. Captain Dorr ... now in the *Ida* at Valparaiso, has lost one or two whole crews to the privateers of the country. It is the most distressing situation that one can be placed in to encounter obstacles that cannot be surmounted by any exertions of one's own.

"The hope of acquiring during the present voyage the means of placing you in a comfortable and independent situation has prompted me to encounter difficulties and toils without the least reluctance—how far my efforts will be crowned with success time alone can only make known. Although I have met with but little encouragement, I shall not cease to struggle for success in the end.

"P.S. Next week the declaration of Independence, which has lately been made, will be celebrated here and I suppose throughout all the Province of Chile that is now in the possession of the Patriots.

"P.P.S. March 8th—To my great consolation on the 5th instant, Captains Davis, Ebbets & Whittemore arrived here, from whom I shall get another crew and proceed to the Marquesas. Adieu, my Dearest Mary, until it shall please an indulgent Providence to permit us to meet again."

Back to the Marquesas Islands
April – June, 1818

Free at last to leave Chile, the *Sultan* set off for another stop at the Marquesas. This time the visit would be sad.

In addition to carrying her replacement crew, the *Sultan* also had a passenger, Reynolds' longtime friend and colleague Captain Isaac Whittemore. Whittemore was a veteran of the Northwest Coast run, having sailed as mate with Captain William Sturgis in 1803. As captain of the *Avon*, Whittemore had sailed from Boston in

1815 as had the *Sultan*, and now they endured the same delay in Chile. But Whittemore had been in ill health for some months. The *Avon* was sold in Coquimbo, and the ailing captain took passage with Reynolds.

On the afternoon of April 16, Reynolds began to work out of the Bay of Coquimbo, bound for the Marquesas.

"Remarks 16 April, 1818—
   "Began with dull foggy weather and calms—Capt. W. H. Davis & Capt. Thomas Meek called on board at the time of our getting under way."

"Remarks 21 April, 1818
   ". . . We hauled on the wind until 4 a.m. when the Island of St. Felix was seen bearing WNW, for which we bore down and at 7 hove to off the north part of it and proceeded in her with Mr. Newell to the shore with an expectation of finding seal, while the Ship continued to lay off and on. Captain Whittemore did not appear so well today as formerly . . . determined to land in the morning with two boats' crews, as the quantities of seal seen was thought an object worth the time that was likely to be consumed in taking

them . . . In consequence of the bad landing and the shyness of the seal, we only, with all hands, were fortunate enough to take 20. During the night the weather turned cloudy with light squalls and fine drizzling showers. It had been my intention to touch at the Gallipagos Islands after leaving St. Felix, but I was informed by Mr. Downes that armed schooners from Lima patrolled that area to capture American vessels. In consideration of this news I determined on proceeding directly for the Marquesas, with the watch employed cleaning seal skins and stretching them. Captain Whittemore continues very low and sick . . . At 10 hours 30 minutes A.M. the Long'de by several distances of the Moon with the Sun was 88 degrees West."

On May 3 Reynolds recorded that Whittemore continued his dysentery and nervous symptoms, and was "quite insensible." Two weeks away from the Marquesas, he wrote:

"Remarks 4 May, 1818—
    ". . . At a few minutes before 6 A.M. departed this life Captain Isaac Whittemore, in the 38th year of his age—he had been in declining state for many months before he came on board the Ship—whether his disorder was consumption, the Dropsy or the Scurvy we could never ascertain,

but he bore it all with uncommon fortitude. He was put in a Hogshead of rum, that he might be preserved until we could reach the land. Lat'de by observation 15 South."

Several days later Reynolds took an account of Whittemore's property and put it in three trunks, after giving sea clothes and bedding to Whittemore's servant and the ship's cook as reward for their attention to him in his sickness.

The *Sultan* made steady progress toward the Marquesas, the Captain marking her position by the stars.

"Remarks 15 May 1818—
"... Long'de by 3 sets of the distances on each side of the Moon with the Stars Regulus and Antares was 132/53 W. The weather for the past 24 hours indicated the vicinity of land, although we saw no birds except the Man-of-war, and those not plenty. Employed airing bedding and clothes."

"Remarks 21 May 1818—
"... Ship laying off NW side of Magdalena ... in the course of the afternoon we were visited by a number of canoes from the Shore from whom we purchased some Potatoes and fresh fish."

The ship *Borneo,* direct from Boston, appeared with Captain Clark, and Caleb made arrangements to meet him at Nuku Hiva, the major Marquesan island. This was the George Clark who had been second mate with Reynolds aboard the *Pearl* a decade earlier. Captain Clark was en route to Norfolk Sound.

The object of this second Marquesas visit was again sandalwood, even though Reynolds had reported carrying fifty tons of it at Coquimbo.

"Remarks 24 May 1818—

". . . Newell returned with a boat load of hogs and brought with him Charles Payson, a trader from Boston, and the principal Chief of the Valley, who had treated Mr. Newell with attention and kindness. I made him a present of a Red Coat and a Short Cutlass. Also here got a load of wood . . . my friend Tapatunee the Chief called and informed me his wood was ready, and that day we brought off upwards of a ton of wood—and two hogs. Proceeding to Nooehuwah we bought 1500 pounds of wood for three muskets, these apparently scarce and the people very indifferent about trading. The next lot of wood I bought with pigs."

"Remarks 1 June 1818—

"Began with fine pleasant weather . . .
through the night squalls and showers of rain. At
8 AM the Ship *Indus* of Salem entered the Bay &
soon after the *Lion* of Providence, Capt. Townsend, last from the Coast of Chili, the former for
sandalwood and the latter for fire wood and water."

On June 6, Reynolds directed Mr. Downes
and two of the crew to dig the grave for Captain
Whittemore.

". . . The place I have selected is the hill on
which Captain Porter U.S.S. *Essex*, had his fortifi-
cation.   At 10 A.M. we left the ship, having
formed a procession, with our own and the boats
of the *Indus*, proceeding toward the Shore with
the last remains of Captain Whittemore for inter-
ment—both ships firing minuet Guns as we pulled
in shore. A large crowd of the natives met us at
the grave and continued with us until the Cere-
mony of burying had closed. Captain Vandeford,
his officers and the greatest part of his crew attended, giving in the most kind and cheerful manner every assistance in his power."

Reynolds erected this sign at the grave:

"Captain Isaac Whittemore, late of the Ship Avon of Boston, who died on 4th May, 1818, aboard Sultan. A Boston Patriot."

Upon reaching Dominica he sent two boats to shore with orders to "bring off the King of the place—whom I detained; my idea in this was to recover the pay for three muskets which himself and tribe had stolen from us last August." With the king in irons, the natives soon supplied the *Sultan* with 2,300 pounds of wood and 9 hogs. The King was set free, and presented with a red coat.

Over the next few days they shipped 5,400 pounds of wood for a total of 7 muskets, always in the meantime "obtaining an ample stock of fruit from day to day." Now Reynolds had enough wood from the Marquesas, which together with what King Kamehameha owed him would suffice at last for Canton. He proceeded to the Sandwich Islands, but his departure for Canton would again be delayed.

At the Sandwich Islands
July – November, 1818

On June 26, 1818, the ship quit the Marquesas, sighting the island of Hawaii only three weeks later. On the east coast, Reynolds endeavored to hold his position in the face of changing winds and squally weather to find anchorage. When he did so, and found the watering place, he called it "the most convenient I have ever seen among the Islands; I was not permitted to water without paying for it nor to buy hogs without first obtaining license from the King. In a brisk canoe trade ... the fruit and vegetables were at a tolerable dear rate."

But his destination was the west coast of Hawaii, there to do business with the King, claiming the large order of wood promised him nine months before.

"Remarks Sunday, 19 July, 1818
". . . By daylight we had only got abreast of Tocaigh Bay between 6 & 7 am—he wind sprung up from the East'd . . . and soon increased to a fresh Gale that obliged us to hand our Top Galt sails and single the Topsails, but by 8 it began to slacken and soon after became calm . . . only to

breeze up from the West'd which obliged us to make several tacks in order to weather the Point of Kyrooah which at Noon bore about 8 miles . . . I was informed by some of the natives who came up in their canoes that the King was there in the village of Kyrooah.

"Remarks Monday, 20 July, 1818
    "Began with light westerly winds with which we stood to the South'd along the shore until we had opened the village of Kyrooah, the present residence of the King, and as my business lay altogether with him I hove to at 3 PM and went with the Boat and called on the King. I met with Doctor Elliot and Mr. Young."

Elliott advised him that a ship called *Liberty* had been sold to the King, but all captains touching at the islands should be aware that the *Liberty* was actually the *Santa Rosa* whose crew had stolen her at Coquimbo. The King, hearing of the illegal owners, ordered the sails unbent and taken on shore, and dispersed the crew.

"Remarks Tuesday, 21 July, 1818
    ". . . A messenger arrived . . . informing me that the King would be here in the morning. This day paid off and discharged from the Ship the natives that had been employed on board for the last

year past. Then informed that the King will not arrive today."

Kamehameha continued to require the traders to follow him here and there, or to wait at his whim. The crew was employed scraping and preparing the ship for paint and varnish before sailing to Canton. Eventually Reynolds was

". . . well received by the King, who assured me that he would soon be at Karakakooa where he would deliver me the wood which I had bought when I was last at Tocaigh . . . While at Kyrooah I was informed by Mr. Elliot that Owen, the Person who deserted from me at St. Catherine's . . . is now on this Island and was one of the Mutineers of the *Liberty*, and that he had threatened to shoot me if ever I should come his way."

"Remarks Monday July 27 1818—
". . . Discharged and paid Ebenezer Clark at his request . . . At 9 am. the King arrived from Kyrooah & took up his residence. Mr. Elliot and Mr. Young came onboard with an invitation from the King for me to go onshore. After calling on his majesty we returned to dinner on board, intending after dinner to begin weighing and taking on the wood."

Weighing and loading the wood occupied the crew for almost a week.

"Remarks Thursday 6 August, 1818—

". . . We acquired a small boatload, 7 piculs, of wood, brought on board in payment for Copper sold to the King, being that obtained at Pitcairn's Island . . . some crew given brief shore leave . . . all hands employed painting. Although I had Tabooed the Ship for the purpose of keeping the Natives away while painting, I was honoured with a visit from some of the King's family and many of the principal Chiefs."

"Remarks 15 August, 1818—

". . . Employed in various jobs preparatory to getting underway.

". . . It will not be improper to observe that in consequence of the want of a sufficient number of men to man the Ship, I had accepted the services of 5 or 6 seamen of the crew of the *Liberty*, whose conduct had been orderly and correct since their arrival here, for their passage to Macao or Canton.

". . . We were visited by Captain Bouchard, who requested that I would have my Ship's company called aft, that he might ascertain if any of the *Liberty* crew were onboard. Those belonging to her not obeying the call, permission was given for them to search in any part of the Ship. They soon after were discovered and were carried on board the Patriot Ship and confined in Irons. Both ships then bore away for Karakakoa Bay and came to anchor in our old station in nearly 12 fathoms water.

". . . Agreeable to an invitation from Captain Bouchard of the Patriot Ship *Argentina* I went on Board for dinner where we spent an agreeable afternoon. The commander requested that I do him the favor of accompanying him the next morning to Kerooa, as he wisht to pay to the King a complimentary visit preparatory to his demand of the *Liberty* . . . I received of the Captain a Present of Sugar and Tobacco."

Bouchard asked Reynolds to remain with him a few days until he could adjust his business with the King, after which he would purchase all the liquors that Reynolds had to spare, together with flour and vinegar and other articles. Reynolds waited several days expecting to receive a load of wood from Bouchard in payment for the rum and other stores. But Bouchard in turn was waiting for his wood. During this new delay Mr. Downes brought Reynolds a letter informing that by an order of the King he was not to stop at either the island of Maui or Oahu.

"Remarks 2 September 1818—

"... Downes had been very rudely treated by the natives, particularly by one of the King's queens who was walking to and fro before his door, and pusht the muzzle of his musket against him, keeping his finger on the trigger at the same time and threatening to shoot him and every person in the ship.

"Some silly though ill disposed person had told the King that I had landed at Karakakoa some centipedes, the stings of which were poison, that the People might be destroyed by them."

"Remarks 19 September 1818—

"... At 9 PM Ship *Eagle*, Capt. Davis, departed the Harbour, on board whom I had shipped 15 Hhds Molasses and 41 Rice. Ships *Levant* & *Osprey* sail'd for Canton."

Fortunately an understanding was reached, and the unfriendly order was revoked.

"Remarks, 21 September, 1818

". . . We accompanied Bouchard to Mowee where we anchored at Lahaina abreast of the Brick House . . . one of our Timah passengers procured us a good Hog and small quantity of potatoes, for which I gave a large Looking Glass. Bouchard had already received payment in Provisions to the amount of 2,000 dollars. Out of 5 hogsheads of rum, by leakage, we could only fill 4 for Bouchard. During the day I sent the wearing apparel of Capt. Whittemore on shore by Mr. Prince, to be sold by him at Public sale on a commission of 3 per cent, together with some remnants of Ship *Avon*, which he brought on board at Coquimbo and left at his death. This day being the Christian Sabbath . . . ship's company had permission to go on shore & spend the day & partake of the amusements of the place."

Now at Oahu appeared the *Mentor*, Captain Suter, and *Brutus*, Captain Nye, from the Northwest Coast, and the *Borneo*, Captain Clarke, from the Marquesas. Another old acquaintance appeared as well, none other than Captain Golovnin of Sitka days, on a Russian frigate bound for Manila. But any sociability was shortlived. For the *Sultan* it was still not possible to leave for Canton.

Mutiny at Oahu

"Remarks 13 November, 1818—At the Sandwich Islands.

".... This evening about 4 o'clock Captain Davis called along side the Ship informing me that the crew of the *Mentor*, Captain Suter, had proceeded to acts of Mutiny and Violence. I immediately manned a Boat, accompanied by Mr. Newell the chief officer, and Mr. Hairbottle the Pilot of the Harbour, having armed ourselves with Cutlasses and Pistols, proceeded to the *Mentor*. On coming alongside the Ship I was informed by Capt. Suter that some of my people had carried off Eight of his Ship's company, who had left his Ship in a state of Mutiny and in defiance of his authority. Notwithstanding the orders of Captain Suter to the contrary, his people went on shore in the Long Boat of the *Sultan*, where they took shelter in a House of one of the Natives. Our Boats which had come to the assistance of Captain Suter proceeded to the shore with all possible dispatch and went in quest of the Mutineers, but to no purpose.

"The Masters of the different vessels then present went to the Shore and called on the Governing Chief of the Island, and made him acquainted with what had taken place. The Chief immediately sent out parties in search of them, and in a short time afterwards found the House which they taken shelter in, immediately surrounded it and sent back a Person to acquaint those who were in search that they were found.

"Accordingly, Captains Suter, Davis and Nye, together with Messrs. Mason and Prince and myself, on approaching the place, found them all together in a small enclosure beyond the door of the House, armed with heavy clubs which they brandished in a most threatening manner, declaring that they would kill the first that should attempt to take them. At the same time, one of them threw a large billet of wood, which passed between Mr. Prince and myself, upon which we rusht on them and in a few moments they were overpowered and secured by binding their hands, but not until several of them were wounded, as were also Captain Suter and Mr. Prince.

"At first we only supposed them armed with clubs, but it was soon known that they had 2 cutlasses and a pistol. Between 10 and 11 o'clock that evening, Capt. Suter returned on board his own ship, taking with him all those of his people who had deserted his Ship. During the night or the remainder of it, all still and quiet.

"During the latter part of the day, I gave a little wholesome chastisement to Joseph Lockwood, who has been a short time on Board the Ship, for encouraging, aiding and assisting Captain Suter's people in

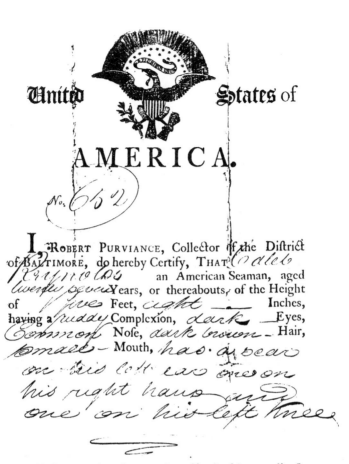

United ᚱtates of
A M E R I C A.

No. 652

I, ROBERT PURVIANCE, Collector of the District of BALTIMORE, do hereby Certify, THAT *Caleb Reynolds* an American Seaman, aged *twenty seven* Years, or thereabouts, of the Height of *five* Feet, *eight* Inches, having a *ruddy* Complexion, *dark* Eyes, *common* Nose, *dark brown* Hair, *small* Mouth, *has a scar on his left ear one on his right hand and one on his left knee*

has this Day produced to me Proof in the Manner directed in the act, entitled, "An act for the Relief and Protection of American Seamen," and pursuant to the said act, I do hereby Certify, that the said *Caleb Reynolds* is a Citizen of the *United States* of *America.*

IN WITNESS WHEREOF, I have hereunto set my Hand and Seal of Office, this *Nineteenth* Day of *September* in the Year One Thousand Eight Hundred and One.

Reynolds' Citizenship Paper, 19 September. 1801

Burned Log of the *Pearl,* 1804-1807

A.A. Baranov

V.M. Golovnin

King Kamehameha
Hawaii

Chief Katlean
Sitka

Nas Arch Angel August 6th 1810

Captain Gollovin & Lieutenant
Rickord of H. J. Russian Majesty's ship
Diana, by a particular favor of the
Author Mr Renald, had perused with
mental pleasure the manuscript of his
truly "interesting Poem" the Sailors Elysium "
request that the following number of
Copies of it, might be sent them to Russia
by Captain Wm Davis's favor, who with
his wonted Civilities has offered his services
on this occasion.

To be directed on Captn Gollovin's or Rickord's
name, to the directors of the Russian American
Company in St Petersbourg.

Copies

William Gollovin _____ 2

Peter Rickord _ _ _ _ 2

Andrew Klebnicoff Master _____ 2

Order Form for "The Sailor's Elysium", Sitka, August 6, 1810

Copy
1

Elia Roodacoff Lieutenant —
Reinhold Brandt — — 1.
     medico Chir:
Jacob Yakooshkeen Midchipman 1.
Necandr Fielatoff Midchipman — . — . 1
Dmitrie Vartavroff — — . — . 1

William H Davis — — 20 Copies
George Sproul Salad — 10 Copies
His Excellency Alexander Barinoff
Governour Russian American Company
& Knight of the order, of St Ann — 20 Copies
Tonnes Engevalsen — — 2 Copies —
Jonathan Winship Jr — 20 Copies
John Ebbetts — — 20 Copies
George W Eayrs — — — 20 Copies
William Lincoln — . — . 10 Copies

Ship Fidelia – at Sea Lat: 39.10, Longit: 52.26 W. Sept: 4ᵈ 1815 –

My Excellent Mary –

I salute you from the Great expanse of waters with health, and esteem – We had a dreadful Gale on the afternoon, and during the night of the 31ˢᵗ of August – being only one day out – with Cape Cod, and the South Shoal of Nantucket under our lee – But, by the blessings of a Good Providence, we are yet safe – I think it highly probable that we may not have another Gale during the voyage so severe – Since the Gale we have had the weather remarkably fine – the Ship is one of the best I ever sailed in, and have no doubt of her performing the voyage with safty under the care of him who Governs all – Charles is an excellent young man, & I think will do himself honor – I am well satisfied with the officers & crew – but truly we exhibited a pitiful scene 10 or a dozen young men in the Gale crawling about the decks, drencht with rain, and half buried in the billows that were frequently breaking over them – but they are all well but one whom I hope will die of sea sickness –

Letter, Caleb Reynolds to "My Excellent Mary", 4 Sept. 1815

Hawaii, ca. 1810

Pitcairn, ca. 1817

At the Sandwich Islands

Remarks – Thursday 24th April 1817

Began with fresh breezes from the NE with clear weather which continued throughout the day –

The Boat returned in the Evening with a load of water having been detained all day in consequence of the tide –

This day discharged Robert Pilkingham, one of the Islanders which I shiped at Norfolks Sound –

Rec.d of Pitt, or Crymakoo, 6 more Hogs with some Farrah soon after –

Remarks – Friday 25th April 1817

Began with fresh breezes from the ENE with continued so during the day

At Evening the Boat returned with the last load of water – so that I had no inducement to stop accept the transaction of some business with Capt. Lewis –

Although the principal object I had in coming here was to take a small Gang of Sealers with Mr Navarra at their head, who was to have them engaged & ready on my arrival here which I was told would have been in Feb. or March – however I found that he had not engaged any & that he appeared rather indifferent about the business & that to wait longer would only prove an unprofitable waste of time – I therefore determined to run up to Owyhee & there endeavour to get what few people I might want –

Through the course of this afternoon Mr Innes found Charles Gibson conveying Rum from the store room in a Bladder, for which we punished him in the evening –

Williams Home, Dighton, Massachusetts

The Children of Caleb and Mary Reynolds

Charlotte, 1829-1920

Samuel, 1820-1867

Joel Barlow, 1826-1851

Joel Barlow Reynolds, 1851-1940

A View of the Island of Nukahiva

Anchorage on the China Coast

making their escape to the shore and for declaring in my presence and in my hearing that we would not drive anyone out of the Boat or knock them down for getting into her. Captain Suter was of the opinion that William Boardman was the person whom he required to leave the Ship at the beginning of the affray and said to him, 'You see, young man, the trouble that I am in.' "

"Remarks Sunday, 22 November, 1818—
   ". . . took in the Long Boat, all hands working on rigging, Pilot came on board and we made sail over the Bar, where we lay to awaiting Captain Suter and *Mentor* with whom I had agreed to keep company to China for mutual safety.

"Remarks 23 November, 1818—
   "At 4 pm, the west point of Whoahoo bore NWN and Diamond Hill ENE 6 Leagues distant. Heavy rain, thunder, lightning. No obsn. Lat'de by account 20/56 N."

To Canton
November 1818 – April 1818

Reynolds was at last en route to Canton with his hard-won cargo of sandalwood. Probably the cargo included a few seal skins and perhaps otter from the long ago days of 1816 when the *Sultan* first set out on the Pacific. In about a month she would enter Macao Roads and await the whim of the Cantonese traders, spending another three months to complete a new cargo for Boston.

Accompanied by the ship *Mentor* and Captain Suter, Reynolds left the Sandwich Islands in a "moderate wind with considerable sea." They would sail for thirty-eight days before reaching Macao and being led up the river to the trading factories at Whampoa. During that month Reynolds weathered a gale "such as I have never witnessed," and battled increasing hazards such as a serious leak in the ship, damaged sails, and the problem of shifting cargo.

"Remarks 24 November, 1818—

". . . Found the *Mentor* had the superiority in sailing by the greatest part of her studding sails . . . Shift load of wood to improve sailing, saw *Mentor*'s light during the night, by noon gained on her. Latitude 20/5N, ship leaks more than usual. Favorable weather allowed drying of potatoes.

"Remarks 2 December 1818—

". . . This day in the order of our accounts of time is Tuesday, the 1st of December, but in our progress westward to the Meridian opposite Greenwich to which Meridian our Nautical Tables are all calculated, and in order that our time should correspond with those Tables, and having gained 12 hours in absolute time, I have advanced our account one day forward and called the Long'de EAST, having by my account of the Long'de passed the 180 degree yesterday."

In the next few days the captain and crew were occupied in the usual tasks of overhauling muskets and "my own pistols and side-arms," filling musket cartridges, making and mending sails, cleaning sandalwood. They began to see quantities of birds, among them an albatross. But nearing land they encountered violent gales.

"Remarks 18 December 1818—

". . . Acquired 1 gallon paint oil from Capt. Suter by means of a line astern, to which attached a cannister."

"22 December—Weather dark and rainy, squally. Sails down in case bad weather, *Mentor* close by."

"23 December—At 1 PM the wind shifted into the NNE and soon increased to a fresh gale—took in all the light sail, rigged in the studding sail boom. At 5 PM close-reeft the Mizen and double reeft the Top and Main Topsails, furl'd main sail and spanker—got down the Fore Top Galt yard and flying sail boom. Bent the storm stay sails and sat them—close reeft the Top Sails. At 5 hours 30 minutes lost sight of *Mentor*. Thick cloudy weather and strong Gales, which continued incessantly throughout the night with heavy falls of rain.

"At daylight the Gale increased with such violence as to oblige us to take in Top Sail and Main Top Sail and lay under the Storm Stay Sails. The wind blew with such fury that we took in the Foretop Mast. Got down the Main Top Gallant yard and secured everything in the best manner we could. At noon the Gale had in some degree increased, and I was under great apprehension for the safety of the Masts, as I had never witnessed such a gale."

"Remarks 24 December, 1818

"Began with the most violent gales ever witnessed at sea, but which between noon and 4 PM began to abate, still too violent for any but the Mizen stay sail. At 8 AM found the Foresail split, also the Main Top in several places. Excepting the splitting of our sails the only material injury we received was with one sea that broke one of the boards in the Bulwark."

"Remarks 25 December 1818—
    ". . . At 10 AM saw land directly ahead, bearing NW/W at the distance of 10 leagues . . ."

"Remarks 26 December 1818—
    ". . . Fell in with the land sooner than expected, and not wishing to pass Formosa at night, we did not carry a press of sail. Accordingly, got the guns in proper places. At 7 PM, high land of Formosa seen about 12 miles distant. Saw a light on Formosa. B'sun reported rigging covered with sand. Judge being swept nearer land than supposed. Formosa light seen directly astern. Another light more brilliant seen on the weather bow. Examined all compasses and they traversed alike. Light was by this time increased to a great height, carrying up a column of flame to a great distance. It was then I first supposed it to proceed from a volcano on shore. We could also perceive a strong smell like that of burning Horn. The light continued during the whole night."

"Remarks 27 December 1818—
    ". . . High tumbling sea frequently came onboard . . . at half past 8 passed a China fishing boat, the first we had seen, followed by great numbers of them."

"Remarks 29 December 1818—

". . . the Pilot came out from Macao, having been sent by the *Mentor* to meet us. Under all sail, standing for Macao Roads. Cleared all islands and at 10 PM anchored in five fathoms, soft muddy bottom. *Mentor* passed us bound for Whampooa."

In a few days Caleb wrote to Mary, dating his letter as many often do at the beginning of a new year—with the old year's date.

"Canton, January 6, 1818 [sic 1819]
"Dear Mary,

"I only have time to say that I arrived here last Saturday & that I am well having enjoyed during the voyage a very great portion of health. I had the pleasure of receiving a number of letters, none later than 1817. I shall with pleasure comply with the trifling orders you have given.

"I shall have more leisure to write by the *Levant*. Expect to be here two months—but hope shortly after the reception of this to see you, under the protecting hand of Him whose providence has preserved me thus far.

Yours with Love & Esteem

C Reynolds"

"Canton, February 1, 1819
"Messrs Boardman and Pope
"Gentlemen

"I avail myself of an opportunity by the *Mentor* to send another debenture Certificate, being the second that I have transmitted to you—the first by Capt. Cary in the *Levant*. I think it possible that I shall not be able to leave here until the first or second week in March, in consequence of having to wait for the Silks that have been ordered.

"It will not be worthwhile for me to say anything on the amount of the sales here as Messrs. Perkins & Co. will make you fully acquainted with that.

"With much respect & esteem, I remain, Gentlemen,

"Your very faithful servant,

C Reynolds"

"Canton, March 18, 1819
"Dear Mary

"I have only time to say that I am well, & am waiting in daily expectation for the remainder of the cargo. I have had no letters from you later than 1817. I have complied in great measure with the most of your orders contained in those letters. God bless you—I hope to see you in August. Remember me to Father & Mother & to all the Family.

C Reynolds"

Canton to Boston
April – September, 1819

It was April when the *Sultan* departed Canton, standing down the river with the *Enterprise* and John Ebbets in company against the difficult and treacherous area of the South China sea. It required navigation among small, rocky-shored islands with hostile natives, and there was always the weather, with restless tropical squalls and heavy heat.

Mariners had long since chosen the narrow path between Java and Sumatra, the Straits of Sunda, as the shortest route toward the Indian Ocean, the Cape of Good Hope, and home. Adding trouble for Reynolds was a persistent leak in the ship, requiring the pumps to overwork. If that was not enough, a month later his anchor cable broke and the anchor was "hopelessly lost." He bought an anchor from Ebbets for $200, drawn on Boardman and Pope. The log continues:

"Remarks 7 May 1819—

". . . Tides very difficult and changeable. Southern Coast of Java. Got through straits from 10 pm to sunrise. Princess Island S/E to SS/E, southern part of Sumatra. Heaviest fall of rain I ever encountered. Employed putting away and securing wood on deck. Lat'd 7/33 South. All sails down in squall. Mr. Dawes very unwell. Crew employed repairing sails and making new ones. Ship *Ophelia*, Capt. Duson in company."

Once through the Straits the *Sultan* sailed into the Indian Ocean, attended by many squalls, and was almost another month reaching the east coast of Africa and rounding the Cape of Good Hope, only to be forced off course in the South Atlantic by more bad weather.

"Remarks 18 June 1819—

". . . From the great disagreement of the Lat'de by Dead Reckoning and that by obsn, we must have been carried to the Southward upwards of 35 miles."

"Remarks 20 June 1819—

". . . Broached a barrel of beef put up in Whampoa, found it very good. Clear and pleasant, scarcely difficult to give the ship steerage way."

"Remarks 21 June, 1819

"... I could not help viewing this day as one of those that frequently preceed bad weather, which I had long expected to meet here, particularly as this is the time of the winter solstice and near the changing of the moon. At 8 pm a gentle breeze . . . having attached a Hook to the head line, had the good fortune to take a very fine Cod or Haike."

Then came a South Atlantic storm, with winds that increased to a violent gale and Reynolds took in all sail. The storms continued two weeks, with no change in sight. When they finally crossed the equator and approached St. Paul Rocks, on the coast of Brazil, they sighted a strange ship.

"Remarks 26 July 1819—

"... At 1 pm, being within hailing distance of the stranger . . . she proved to be French Ship *Archimides* of Havre de Grace, commanded by Captain Bunker, formerly of Nantucket, 71 days out from Valparaiso . . . Captain Bunker very obligingly supplied us with a Barrel of Pork, some vegetables and lamp oil. Arranged to pay his wife in Nantucket in October. At 5 pm parted company, rainy and cloudy."

"... From Captain Bunker I received the following information: That in April last, the Town of Guasco, on the coast of Chile, had been totally destroyed by an Earthquake, but fortunately the inhabitants had sufficient notice to escape the dreadful destruction that awaited them, with the exception of 6 or 7 who perished in the ruins of the falling dwellings.

"... That Patriots had possession of the whole Province of Chile, with the exception only of the Town and Harbour of Boldivia ... that there were laying at Valparaiso upwards of fifty merchant vessels from different parts of the world at the time the *Archimedes* sailed ... among them US Frigate *Macedonian*, Capt. Downes, who had come, it was supposed, to demand restoration of the American Schooner *Traveller*, Capt. Wilcocks of Philadelphia and the Brig *Cossack* of Boston, Capt. Myrick, captured at Quimas."

After the July news from Chile there are no entries in Reynolds' log until late August, east of the Virgin Islands. Here the Captain wrote, "This is the hottest day I ever felt."

In the heat he sighted another strange ship, this time suspecting a privateer. He changed course to avoid her, then lost her in the haze. He sighted and avoided several more strange, distant sails as he passed Bermuda, then nearing Nantucket began a series of soundings every half hour.

> "Remarks 2 September 1819—
> "... As I supposed the ship to be on the NE edge of Nantucket Bank, when the soundings corresponded, and wishing to get into the Channel as soon as possible to avoid the dangers to be presented on the Nantucket side, I steered off ENE and NE, expecting every hour to deepen the waters—being uncertain even of the Lat'de."

All day the soundings read only 20 to 30 fathoms, then rose to 40, as the ship was gradually wrapped in fog.

> "Remarks 3 September, 1819—
> "... The fog having at last cleared I sighted a small sail to leeward two or three points on the bow, ran down and spoke to her, proved to be a fishing boat from the Cape—supplied us with a half barrel of Macerell. At the same time sounded 60 fathoms, at half past 2 made sail."

At evening the thick returning fog was accompanied by fresh gales, but near midnight it cleared and Reynolds sounded in 100 fathoms. By noon the next day he sighted Cape Cod bearing NW, at 42/8 North.

The *Sultan* was home again.

Once at anchor Reynolds received this letter, which confirms the trust placed in the captain by the owners, and suggests security problems at the ports.

"Boston, Augt. 4th, 1819   Ship *Sultan* of Boston
"Captain Reynolds, Sir
    "We are now daily expecting your arrival—We have particular reasons for requesting you not to show your Bills of Lading, Manifest or any other papers until you see us, to any person who may board you, nor answer any questions regarding who has property on board.
    "If you are asked where any particular property is stowed do not answer, and do not let any person go below with a view of looking at Marks if any can be seen. Do not deliver your letters until you see us.

"If you are boarded by any Custom House Officer, who asks for your Manifest, be sure he is one, before you show it, and we would rather you put him off by any excuse if you can, but if he insists upon one, do not show him any Bills of Lading or papers, except the Ship's regular papers.

"Let us know of your arrival, if you can before it is generally known. Our Mr. Pope lives where he did when you left.

Yr. Obt. Servant, Boardman and Pope
"Do not let your officers answer any questions.

"In your Manifest see that all the property shipped by Sturgis & Co. in which we are concerned is consigned to us only—do not let any other name appear."

CHAPTER SIX

Dighton
1820

"Tho distant, Dighton, still thy stream . . .
I trace the summits first to you"

Reunited at last with his Mary after four arduous years at sea, the captain now spent several months of treasured time in family company in Dighton, enjoying a well earned rest and writing about his travels.

While another trading voyage in less than a year would take him again to Chile, Reynolds would never again travel to the Sandwich Islands where he had spent so much time and made many friends. Nor would he again sail near Pit-cairn Island. He would not revisit the Northwest Coast, nor the Columbia River and California's deep bays.

Of all these places he wrote at length, provid-ing personal insights of the world as it was when young America burst into the maritime trade.

The world had first learned of the Pitcairn settlement in 1808, when Matthew Folger, in the American sealing ship *Topaz* came upon the is-land and its inhabitants. Details of the story were gradually being added to world knowledge, and Reynolds had his own first-hand account to tell. In a long letter addressed to an author unknown to us, the captain enlarged upon the entries he had made in his *Sultan* log.

"Adams by the year 1800 was left with the sole care of the women and children. From this period, I presume, he began that system of Industry, Moral-ity & Religion which he so happily established in his little Colony . . . one of their houses was set apart for public worship, where he assembled his little family twice each Sunday for that purpose . . . To all ques-

tions which I put to them they answered in English,
which they spoke sufficiently well to be well understood, and spoke the Otaheitian tongue as well . . .
they beheld us in unlimited confidence, for they had
not yet been taught by shameful experience that dis-
simulation & distrust formed a part of the prudent
maxims of Civilization . . . the first thing enquired
for by these young men on coming aboard was Spelling books, if they were the means of learning to
read."

"Adams came aboard at my request . . . while
the boats were employed in bringing off the provisions he prepared for us. He appeared to be much
delighted with his visit, it being the only time he had
been onboard of a Ship since he landed from the
Bounty. I asked him but few questions respecting the
mutiny, not wishing to pursue . . . too far . . . a subject unpleasant to him. The mutiny took place in the
early part of the morning watch . . . he did not point
out any particular circumstance . . . but attributed it
to general disaffection . . . I asked if he wished . . .
some suitable person might be sent to assist in the
education of the children. He did not like the propo-
sition and replied with emotion, 'I thank you not to
do so for I never wish to see any person come here
for any such purposes while I live.'

"I received a very reasonable supply of hogs,
goats, & poultry, together with yams, tarrah,

sugar cane ... To their farm stock of vegetables I
was only able to add the seeds of melons and beans
... During the residence of the present occupants
of the Island, vestiges of a former population have
been discovered, including a morai . . . Yams,
sugar cane and the cloth tree were found growing
at the time when the Bounty arrived there . . . I
never saw one of the Islanders sit down to eat or
lie down to sleep without first invoking the bless-
ing of their Creator."

Word could not yet have reached Reynolds in
Dighton that a month after his return to America
his friend King Kamehameha died. The 1819 death
of this all-powerful Hawaiian king brought vast
changes to the islands. The King's sons canceled all
tabus, including the monopoly of the sandalwood
trade, and allowed the various chieftains to trade
alone. The greedy chieftains sent dozens of men into
the forests and before long the sandalwood supply
was depleted. Within a year the relaxation of the
King's tabus spread confusion, disorder and demor-
alization among the people, setting the stage for
strange new visitors—the New England missionar-
ies. Their influence, together with that of the whal-
ers who now dominated Pacific trade, changed for-
ever the basic society of the islands.

Reynolds' *"Historical Notes on the Sandwich Islands, Taken in 1806, from Tradition and Observation,"* is a scholarly discourse on the islanders' government, religion, agriculture, and daily activities.

On Cannibalism: "It was the opinion of those who first visited these islands that the inhabitants were cannibals; they had much reason for that belief in the affair of Captain Cook . . . In a conversation I had with some of the natives, who accompanied us to the Northwest coast of American in 1805, they appeared to be struck with horror at the imputation of such practices, and asked if that was the custom with us."

On Human Sacrifice: "Mr. Young, who has resided with them more than 20 years, told me it was never a popular custom with them to offer up human sacrifices to the Gods . . . happening only once during his residence . . . when the close of the war an offering was made at the Morai of twelve men slain in battle plus hogs and vegetables . . . but not an instance of a prisoner sacrificed to satiate the appetite of man or discharge a duty to their Gods."

On Bathing: "In no country, I believe, is the indulgence of natural desires so common as here; yet that dreadful attendant on promiscuous enjoyment which has markt its way through other countries was

a stranger here until introduced by the first visitors.
That this disorder should never have made its appearance may be, indeed, owing to their habit of bathing
. . . the particular amusement of both sexes, and of all
conditions. They are, in this useful and pleasant exercise, expert in the extreme. Altho I have visited these
islands several times, yet I have never heard of an instance of any person drowning, tho they are frequently upset in their canoes a great distance from
shore."

On Food: "They salt their pork, procuring the
salt by evaporation of sea water, but prefer their fish
raw . . . They bake or steam vegetables underground,
which they afterwards knead into a pudding or paste,
and dilute it with water . . . This preparation they call
"Poie" which after it has undergone a moderate fermentation, is both pleasant and nutritive. Strangers
soon become fond of it, and many have acknowledged its excellent qualities in restoring to the stomach its proper tone, and repairing injured constitutions . . . From the Tie root, exquisitely sweet . . . by
the assistance of some foreigners residing among
them they make a strong distilled liquor resembling
in taste and smell an indifferent gin . . . They have
several kinds of wood, some which will answer for
Ship timber or cabinet wood, but the Tappa or cloth
tree is most valuable, and is planted and tended with
great care. The grounds appropriated for its growth
are enclosed on the East with a high fence of 18 or 20

feet to defend it from the morning sun and easterly
wind . . . from its bark they make all their clothes,
oiling, glazing and also painting and staining it in
very beautiful and brilliant colors."

On their Persons: "Situated as they are between
the tropics, it would be natural to suppose they cannot stand the cold of higher latitudes . . . I have had
sufficient instances to the contrary. We had six of
these men on board the Ship on the Northwest
Coast of America, for a period of sixteen months,
between the parallels of 55 degrees and 56 degrees of
North Lat'de, and in all instances they performed
with as little complaint as our seamen . . . it may depend, I think, on bodily constitution and texture of
skin, which renders them impervious to the cold
. . . the texture is widely different from the inhabitants of Africa and their descendants in America, who
in all exercise sweat freely . . . this is not the case with
these islanders, neither is there anything offensive in
their smell."

On the Future: "I think it not improbable that
His Pacific Majesty, for so I shall call him, will in the
course of a few years attempt a commercial intercourse with the Russian American Company established at Norfolk Sound, in which he may supply
them with Beef, Pork, and vegetables, and at no distant time with Sugar and Rum. He had already,
from the stock which Capt. Vancouver left him, an
abundant stock of cattle; and pork was ever been the

principal animal food of the Islands. They manufacture an excellent kind of cordage suitable for the running rigging of Ships, from the bark of a tree, also small line from a species of hemp equal to anything I have ever seen of the kind. Tobacco may also become an article of trade."

His writing was interrupted when another sailing assignment called him away from Mary and home, even before the birth of their expected first child.

At the end of May he traveled to Rhode Island, hired by Edward Carrington & Co. of Providence as captain of the ship *Fame*. A week later the ship departed, bound for Gibraltar, Batavia and Chile.

The work of this his final voyage would be the buying and selling of commodities across the southern Pacific and would not require a desperate search for the once vital sea otter and sandalwood. On this voyage, however, he would face the most severe test of his skill and faith.

CHAPTER SEVEN

Ship *Fame*
1820-1822

". . . I now thought that all our efforts were in vain,
and that we must perish . . ."

The *Fame* left Providence bearing the usual
cargo list plus several bills of lading for ports afar.
A typical one:

"31 May, 1820 —Bill of lading:
 "Shipped in good order and well-conditioned
by Cyrus Butler and Edward Carrington & Co. in
and upon the ship called the *Fame* whereof is Master, for the present Voyage Caleb Reynolds now
in the Harbour of Providence bound for Europe
or elsewhere . . . twenty-one cases Muskets,

137

twenty-eight hundred seventy one barrels flour, thirty half barrels flour, one hundred fourteen barrels beef . . . to be delivered, in the like good order and well-conditioned, at the aforesaid port of Europe or elsewhere (the danger of the seas only excepted) by Caleb Reynolds and Wm. S. Wetmore, joint super-cargoes onboard."

"Remarks 3 July, 1820—
    ". . .For several days heavy swells, overcast, similar to most days so far across Atlantic, frequent lightning, squalls and rain.

"Remarks 4 July, 1820—
    ". . . This morning saw a swallow . . . this being the 4th of July, observed it as a national festival.

"Remarks 7 July, 1820—
    ". . . asserted by some that they could smell in the breeze the fragrance of wild flowers on shore . . . by an experiment we made by dropping a ball of ashes in the water, the current sat to the SE . . . eleven sail of vessels in sight this day."

When the *Fame* reached Gibraltar in early July they spent three weeks in trade, nine days of it just unloading the cargo of flour. During this stop *Fame* spoke to the *Overembo* and *Philip* of

Baltimore and the *Union* of Providence. The schooner *Fenilon* and the *Union* took letters to America for Reynolds. Unfortunately, there were also five desertions at Gibraltar. Allowed to go ashore, several crewmen did not return as promised.

As the ship sailed south then east to round the Cape of Good Hope, the crew was employed making sennit and picking oakum—respectively a ship's important braided rope and strands of hemp for caulking. By November they anchored at Batavia, and traded in this area of Java until the spring of 1821 when the ship set out across the Pacific toward Chile, encountering fierce weather and near disaster.

"Remarks 4 June, 1821—
". . . Heavy squally weather with rain, the clouds constantly gathering to windward & increasing in strength, sharp lightning in almost every point of the horizon. It streamed in constant flashes, accompanied by heavy thunder. The darkness became awful & the lightning for some moments would deprive us of sight . . . At 3 am passed over one of the most tremendous squalls of thunder, lightning, hail and rain that I have experi-

enced . . . in this tempest I observed the Iron Cap
at the head of the Main Top Galt mast head to be
in a constant light blaze for some minutes."

Remarks 5 June, 1821—
    "This day began with violent hard Gales,
blowing at times squalls with fine rain . . . the Ship
under bare poles with the exception of the fore
top mast stay sail"

Remarks 11 June, 1821—
    "Cloudy weather with spaces of clear sky,
atmosphere filled with haze and vapour. At sunrise the canopy of heaven displayed a scene of the
most sublime grandeur, the eastern clouds were
tinged with gold, below them towards the horizon
appeared blended the colours of brass and steel,
while the Western sky which was spread with
broad fleecy clouds in almost parallel lines crossing each other were painted in rich crimson."

"Remarks 15 June, 1821—
    "Began with heavy gales . . . ship scudding
under the Goosewings of the fore sail, sea began to
rise in mountains. At 4 pm a tremendous sea
struck the ship's stern, broke in one of the false
deadlights and forcing a deluge of water into the
Cabin and carrying away the round house . . . In
an instant Mr. Eddy was on deck and told me the
ship's stern was broken in—I ran below to see
what had taken place and found one of the false

deadlights broken in but the stern otherwise whole . . . ordered the pumps to be tried immediately . . . the lashing of the boats were cut away and oars passed up . . . deadlight repaired by nailing a board, ship fairly free of water, the storm still raging with inconceivable violence and several seas broke against the stern—fortunately it remained secure, the water only coming in through the seams which could not be made tight.

". . . Our only hope was the good qualities which the ship possessed in steering and scudding—it was the last desperate alternative & it happily succeeded, under the guidance of that God who governs the tempest . . . the sea following in mountains, the wheel rope which had been new after we left Sunda, by the constant and severe friction parted the ship—I now thought that all our efforts would prove vain and that we must perish . . . happily she answered the weather helm though laying almost on her side and buried in the billows.

". . . At 6 the wind began to abate but the sea was rolling after us in mountains, which I was fearful would overwhelm us every moment . . . hands were sent up to unbend the top sail, that a spare could go to the yard with all possible dispatch . . . Mr. Renches and Downes by my request got a spar over the stern and prepared some boards to nail over the broken deadlight . . . this task Downes accomplished at the hazard of his life—it was singularly providential that the sea rolled more regular and smooth while he was over the stern than it did for many hours after.

"... We now found that our Medicine Chest was entirely destroyed, all our spare Glass and Crockery, together with our Gun powder & ready filled Cartridges & many of our small stores, besides the injury of the books . . . the sea toward noon began gradually to subside."

"Remarks 23rd June, 1821—
"... an evening clear and delightful, scarcely a cloud floating through the vault above us, the Cross of the South, a beautiful Constellation, beamed its mild lustre through that quarter of the heavens which I could but see as pledges of a fine day."

"Remarks 24 June 1821—
"... this day as been the finest we have had for nearly 40 preceeding."

Caleb had decided to sail northeast of New Zealand instead of south of it, and once clear of its shores he bemoaned the fact that he had no new charts of the area.

"... I could only fall on my former track in the Sultan ... considerable rain, so much we filled up two Casks—this day being the 4th of July & the second that we had passed in the Ship, of course gave our crew as good a dinner as our condition would allow & suspended all duties but those absolutely necessary."

In another month *Fame* anchored safely at Valparaiso. While there is again no record, possibly this was his first chance to receive mail, and perhaps it was here he learned of the birth of his son. His papers do not mention it until he wrote to Mary from New York in June, 1822, saying, "your letter has dispelled every anxious thought, that you are well and so is the boy . . ."

Sailing from Valparaiso up and down the coast of Chile, the ship entered into brisk trading for several months, through March, 1822. Bills of lading show the outbound cargo: cases or bags of flour, wheat, beans, beef, tallow, fish, almonds, butter, bread, soap, cocoas, shoes, and liquor— and silks. The account list shows expenses at Valparaiso for vegetables, fruit and bread, for hiring horses to and from Coquimbo, for paying a boy to retrieve his stolen boat, and to pay a police guard for looking after the crew to prevent desertions.

Meanwhile the captain wrote long letters to friends at home, John Bailey of the United States State Department and Jonathan Leonard of Canton, Massachusetts. A student of political affairs, Reynolds sent both men reports of the revolutionary scene on this his first visit in Chile since 1818. The letters were composed over a period of four or five weeks, as he found time "whenever my peddling duties are suspended."

To Leonard in Massachusetts:
"... To send you an account of what is likely to take place in this part of the new world ... As supposed by our Legislature, man is making rapid strides here towards consummation of his political freedom ... but my dear friend I am led to anticipate a very different result ... had we checked, it would have led us to an axiom of your own: that until the prevalence of bad habit can be removed, the influence of good example can have but little effect ... I can well remember the youthful enthusiasm we felt, inspired by the French Revolution and we have both lived to see & regret its issue, but you will tell me not to despair—my fears are that we will never realize here the republican cause by recognizing the independence of this country. They have in the nature of social institutions everything to learn, with too much pride to

enter the school! All the restrictions which the former Government placed in the way of Commerce are kept in operation by the present, with the additions of many new ones equally discouraging."

To Bailey, in Washington:
"I congratulate you from this distant part of the world on your entry into the department of State . . . I learn here with much satisfaction that the Florida Treaty has been ratified by the Spanish Government, the line however does not extend far enough to the southward to take in the harbour of Port St. Francisco . . . It would have proved a valuable acquisition . . . I cannot but think that it would have been more prudent for Spain, in her present situation, to have ceded to the U. States for a moderate compensation the entire Penninsula, together with all the country to the westward of the Rio Colorado . . . than to have it wrested from her by her revolted subjects, which they are now in a fair way very shortly to accomplish . . . this would remove the possibility of a bad neighbor, an evil we may well expect to encounter at no very distant period.

"I learn here, though have not seen it in print, that the Congress has authorized the President to acknowledge the independence of this country. It is a little mysterious how they caught those sympathetic feelings for this distant nation

. . . had they consulted the traveller or the merchant to learn the true character of this people who no more resemble the population of the U. States in habit, character, or morals, than I do in person the King of Congo.

"The difference . . . is like our Penn and Raleigh compared to Cortes and Pizarro, by whose cupidity and cruelty this fruitful region was drenched in the blood of its ancient inhabitants. Thus I cannot forgive the national legislature for its short sighted policy decision on the Missouri question.

"When I first visited this country in the early part of the revolution my heart was filled with the warmest wishes for its success . . . but experience has dissipated this illusory vision, so consoling to the feelings of the Patriot and the Good man . . . I hope you will . . . believe this is not an admonition to the Government, tho using the very privilege however of railing at its folly.

"I have been fourteen months from the U. States on a trading voyage & last from Batavia . . . we also have it in expectation to visit . . . the western coast of California but cannot hope to see our own starry banner waving over the tranquil waters of St. Francisco and St. Diego . . . I think it highly probable that they will in the course of eighteen months renounce their allegiance to

Ferdinand & accept of new masters . . . this Country would be a Garden to the Columbian River Settlement!

"To illustrate the fact that republican is not the form of government intended here to be adopted & that equal rights are not to be recognized, we have only to glance at the new order of nobility already created, consisting of three grades; they can only be tried for crimes & offences by their peers or equals in rank.

"Before I close this I must give you a specimen of the freedom of the Press in this country, in the case of a young German who is now in exile . . . for publishing a paper on the liberty of the Press, heading it with the very article in their constitution securing that privilege—those who have seen it assure me it was an ingenious, modest, well written paper. He was brought to answer for it . . . and in order to check any further inquiry into the nature of Government, he was banished to the Island of Juan Fernandez, now become the receptacle of state's prisoners and convicts. I would have sent you the paper, though written in Spanish, had it not been suppressed by the Government.

"Again I must express my hopes that the U. States will endeavor, in some future Treaty with the Spanish to possess themselves of the Country to westward of the River Colorada . . . should parts of this letter appear worthy of public notice, I should have no objections with the exception of my name to their being published.

"Your obedient servant, C. Reynolds"

Her trading completed, the *Fame* finally left Chile March 5th, 1822, carrying with her this assignment:

"By H. Blikman, op den Togendam No. 23 Amsterdam:

"Shipped by the Grace of God and in good order and well-conditioned by C. Reynolds & Wm. Wetmore upon the good Ship called Fame whereof is master under God for this present voyage Caleb Reynolds, now riding at anchor in this Harbour and by God's grace bound for New York, one thousand forty-four slubs of Copper, weighing two thousand quintals—ninety-nine pounds . . . eighty-four hides . . . one box & one bag cont. Three Thousand Two Hundred & Fifty Spanish Dollars . . . And so God send the good Ship to her desired Port in safety."

With this valuable cargo, the *Fame* reached the desired port of New York in safety June 20, 1822. Two days later Reynolds wrote to his wife:

"Mrs. Mary E. Williams, c/o N. Williams Esquire
"Collector of the Customs, Dighton, Mass.

"My dearest Mary
     "The day after our arrival at the Quarantine
Ground, I had the unspeakable pleasure & satisfaction of receiving your kind letter, date at Providence 16 May, and also one from brother Thomas,
who I find is now a resident of this city—we were
only detained two days at the Quarantine Ground
. . . I have wrote Mr. Carrington for his permission to leave the ship here, if not I shall have to
remain here until she is discharged. I am in good
health & much better spirits than I have felt for
some time past—your letter has dispelled every
anxious thought, you were well and so was the
boy, for whom I am to purchase School Books—
this will only justify what I had intimated to you
. . . that you were by this time packing him off to
School. Thomas says he is a large fat boy & that
he is clear Williams. I have always had a wish that
he would resemble his mother . . .
     "I hope that you will not come to Provi-
dence to meet me but remain at Dighton where it
will be tranquil . . . our friends will be disappointed in the things from Canton, the voyage
having taken a different turn from that which Mr.
Carrington intimated to me . . . but the happiness
of meeting with you will more than balance any
disappointments in the voyage . . . to kiss and ca-
ress the boy whom you long so much to present

to me, will be a pleasure for which I have so often sighed with fond impatience to enjoy.

"My heart at times is swelled with Gratitude to HIM by whose goodness I have been conducted in safety amidst conflicting elements & the diseases of tropical regions, so fatal to the inhabitants of other climates.

"Give the boy a thousand kisses for Father, who longs to vie with his mother in all the demonstrations of Parental tenderness and affection, who will hasten with all speed to their embraces.

"Dear Girl with the purest devotion I remain yours most affectionately, C. Reynolds"

CHAPTER EIGHT

On Terra Firma
1822-1858

"He will have a nice place to go to school, only a few rods from the house"

Reynolds pursued the necessary business at New York, surely impatient to go to Dighton and no doubt setting a speed record for the journey. One can only imagine his reunion with Mary and his fond embrace and first view of the toddler, Samuel Williams Reynolds, now two years old. The boy was born on 8 June, 1820, one day before the *Fame* set out from Providence.

Once in Dighton, with recommendations from Boardman and Pope, his longtime employers, Reynolds inquired for various further employment. His ideas included the possibility of chartering a ship ". . . for a voyage of two years . . . it would not suit me to purchase a ship and then fit it out, I have only the means of fitting it out on my own . . ." This opportunity did not appear. If he had the means to fit out a ship, he had means to begin a new life on land.

Meantime the captain again set to writing, this time a long letter to Washington, D.C., regarding his 1816 visit to the Columbia River.

"Sir: Presuming from the interest you had taken during the last session of Congress to effect the permanent settlement of the United States at or near the mouth of the Columbia River, and on the probability that the subject would be revived in the session now approaching, I have ventured to offer you such remarks as a short stay in the River enabled me to make.

"On approaching the mouth of the River from the Ocean, an entire chain of broken water is seen stretching from Cape Disappointment to Point Adams, which in standing in to the eastward begins to separate, and soon opens a passage to the north east, leading directly into Baker's Bay the first anchoring place . . . through this channel . . . ships will have four fathoms of water on full tides . . . the shores are moderately high and covered principally with a heavy growth of Pine, Spruce and Hemlock. Oak and Ash timber, it is said, is in great plenty up the River, but none of these trees are seen growing at the mouth. The soil appears good, and would probably produce all the fruits necessary for the sustenance and comfort of man the climate mild and soft compared with places in the same latitudes on the Atlantic side, and is inclined to humidity.

"I was informed by a young man who spent two years with the Chinook tribe, previous to the commencement of the first settlement, that winters were warm and moderate, the snow seldom laying longer than two or three days and frequently dissolving as fast as it fell. The quantity of rain, I should judge from what I saw myself when there in 1816, considerably greater than in the middle states.

"It has been suggested by several of my friends, who have made many voyages there, that the most convenient place for settlement would be at some place within the Straits of Juan de Fuca, at or near Point Protection. The land is more open and free from timber, and would therefore present fewer obstacles to the hand of tillage . . . and in a maritime or commercial view has a decided advantage over the Columbia mouth, with no impediments in the way of entering or departing. The impediments at Columbia, however, in the estimation of military men might be considered as real advantages, as Cape Disappointment terminates in a round hill of considerable altitude . . . and might be so fortified as to render the ingress of an enemy dangerous if not impossible.

"In the event of permanent settlement, independent of the Fur Trade, the Lumber of the country would form a principle article of commerce and find a ready market in most places from California to Chile, those countries almost destitute of timber. But to what extent this trade might be pushed, under the present state of civilization and improvement . . . would be hazardous to conjecture . . . they have hitherto built their houses of unbaked bricks, roughcast with lime and covered with tiles. Even so what timber is needed would be much cheaper and of better quality from Columbia than from their own provinces. From California, rich in grain and cattle, provisions might be drawn for the Garrison & the adventurers which might attend them.

"I am thus particular from a knowledge of the resources of the southern coast countries, having within the last ten or twelve years made several voyages to that coast. But how far the Revolution has affected them I will not pretend to say . . . it would be reasonable to conclude that it has rather promoted than checked industry.

"The Russians have had an establishment on the California coast since 1811, and it flourishes and is capable of defence as to induce the Governor of Monterey to relinquish a project he formed to dispossess them.

"I feel no hesitation in saying that national policy and the increase of our commerce in the Pacific Ocean . . . suggest the importance of a competent Military Establishment on our short territorial limits on the shores of that Ocean."

His letter again expressed his familiar wish that the United States had bargained with Spain for a different boundary. He suggested all the land west of the Colorado River, which would include part of Utah, all of Nevada and California, and of course the fabulous coast from Oregon to Mexico!

Gradually Reynolds turned his thoughts from the sea to buying land. He traveled to New Hampshire, where he had lived briefly before his early voyages, and established residence in Pembroke, leaving his family in Dighton while he bought property in Merrimack County.

In May, 1825, he wrote to Mary, waiting in Dighton:

"I contemplate returning by the first week in June ... Mr. Tallant left me the horse and cow last week, and I have another engaged ... Mr. Leonard writes that he has not engaged me a chaise yet, as none could be procured at 140 dollars, the price I limited him at ... I expect to get one in Haverhill ... I have done nothing to our old house yet & do not contemplate on it until you see it ... I have not yet been to Concord to enquire the price of furniture but intend to go before I leave here. I have the price of a lot of second kitchen things .. . we can decide in Boston whether it will be best to take them. I have all my spring work done except a day or two fencing and planting a few small things in the Garden.

"I never enjoyed better health than since I have been here. I hope that Sam and yourself have been well—he will have a nice place to go to school, only a few Rods from the House. There are now between 80 & 90 students at the Academy.

"Yours with great affection,
C. Reynolds"

Once settled on their new property, which increased eventually to thirteen acres, Caleb and Mary welcomed two more children, a son Joel Barlow and a daughter, Charlotte Stark. The poet Reynolds named this second son for the American Joel Barlow, a government diplomat who was himself a poet. Charlotte's name included Stark for Henry Stark, Caleb's good New Hampshire friend.

Through Stark the captain became a government census agent for New Hampshire and took part in various community affairs.

In 1834 a Stark letter advised Reynolds: "Should you wish to have your son's name entered on the list of Applicants for a Midshipman's appointment, write to the Secretary of the Navy, the same course for the West Point school."

Meantime young Sam wrote to his uncle, Thomas Williams:

"Pembroke, July 13, 1834
    "Respected Uncle: I take this opportunity to write you a few lines which will be handed you by Captain Locke. In the first place I would tell you we are all well. Barlow goes to the academy & I work on the farm but I don't like it. I want to go to sea in the spring for I am not content on shore. I certainly shall go some- time or other."

At seventeen, Sam indeed went to sea, and at age twenty went into business with an import-export company in Philadelphia.

After his 1846 marriage to Emma Cush- man, he formed a similar business, Reynolds and Cushman. Caleb Reynolds then moved with Mary, Barlow and Charlotte to Philadel- phia as well.

While nothing survives of the captain's writing after 1840, he must have continued, given his wont, to comment upon the things he lived to see:

That his 1822 prediction would come true, and we would have to fight not Spain but Mexico for the lands west of the Colorado River;

That what he called the "garden country" along the California coast would become a reality and be settled rapidly, first with the prospectors in the great Gold Rush;

That in his retirement the growing frenzy between the states foreshadowed the conflict that would bracket his years: his life had begun on the eve of a war, and it would end on the eve of another;

That he had seen his nation emerge as a major player in world trade and political power, and that he himself had taken part in the early adventures at sea which made it possible.

At age 87 in Philadelphia, October, 1858, with Mary and daughter Charlotte at his side, the captain, it is said, "went to sleep in his chair."

Author's Notes

Although Reynolds' 1817 Pitcairn visit was next after the two Englishmen of 1814, and though when at home in 1820 he wrote at length about his acquaintance with Adams, the *Sultan*'s visit does not appear in the history books. In the 1930s, with great reluctance, his grandson Joel Barlow Reynolds, at the behest of his sister Emma, sent the precious log to New York for the perusal of Nordhoff and Hall, then engaged in writing about the *Bounty*. They were unimpressed.

Through a correspondence with *National Geographic* magazine's Luis Marden I learned that there was an island register, and that the *Sultan* did appear in it. It noted that one of the island women, known as "Jenny," was anxious to leave Pitcairn, and that the *Sultan* gave her passage. Nothing in Reynolds' log mentions it.

Though Reynolds managed to bring home and preserve not only his 1804 apprentice log but his *Sultan* and *Fame* logs as well, plus letters from Boardman and Pope, and copies of his letters to others—none of Mary's letters survive. He must have treasured them as much or more as the other papers. Mary survived him, and preserved his letters, but hers to him and any photograph of her are lost. Her image is preserved only in the words of his poetry: fair hair and complexion, blue eyes. Perhaps her daughter Charlotte's picture suggests her face.

APPENDIX

Historical Notes of the Sandwich Islands Taken in 1806, both from Observation and Tradition

It is generally understood that Captain Cook was the first European that ever visited these Islands. He discovered Attoi, the westernmost of the group lying in his passage from the Friendly Islands toward Bering Straits, and those situated to the eastward on his return from the northward.

The inhabitants of Attoi, at that time, appeared utterly unacquainted with every European article they saw, excepting Iron, the use of which they were thought to be acquainted with. That a people, thus secluded from the rest of the world, and having no Iron mines among them, should have obtained a knowledge of that article, has remained a mystery, until the present time.

But a concurrence of incidents, which took place this present year, will do away with all further conjecture on the subject, and establish a fact very possible in the nature of things. Captain Sole of the American ship *Taber* on a passage from China toward the coast of Peru, fell in with the wreck of a Japanese Ship; there were eight or ten persons onboard whom he afterward landed on the island of Whaahoo, when I saw them in September, 1806. They were afterward taken to China by Captain Delano of Boston, the same year.

Some time in May this same year, there was driven on shore at the Island of Mowee, a wreck-float. Mr. Hairbottle, a resident of Whaahoo, was sent by the King to take possession of it as his right, a privilege sanctioned by time immemorial, though but few Kings have had the good fortune to seize on such a treasure.

APPENDIX

It was found to consist of seven large pieces of pine timber, each having been formed from several smaller ones, after the manner of mast making. Each one of them had a large sheave or pulley fixed in each end, of about thirty-six inches in diameter and six in thickness, the whole was strongly fastened together with bolts of Iron and Copper. The timber was much eaten by worms, and worn by the surges of the Sea. Mr. Hairbottle having formerly made a voyage to the Northeast of China and Tartary, was struck with the resemblance between the Iron and Copper work of this float, and was of opinion that they were of China or Tartar origin.

Capt. Vancouver, in his voyage around the world, observes that while laying at the Sandwich Islands, the natives had informed him that they had found on their shores large pieces of timber, fastened together with Iron, long before their knowledge of the Europeans; but that these instances had been very rare. He was of opinion that these wrecks were from the coast of America, and were the ruins of bridges which had been washed away by freshets and carried into the gulf of California, and hence into the limits of the Trade Winds, and at last wafted upon these Islands.

But Mr. Hairbottle's opinion has been well established by the testimony of the Japanese who were landed by Capt. Sole, they all appeared to be well acquainted with the use and construction of them, and affirm them to be of Japanese or Tartar origin. It must appear strange and singular that a body, accidentally discharged on the open Ocean, without any directing principle, from the shore of Tartary, should at length reach an Island in the North Pacific Ocean. To account for which it will be necessary to suppose there is a prevailing current, assisted by a prevailing or periodical wind, both setting from the coast of Tartary in a south east direction; until meeting with the general easterly, or Trade winds, and thence borne along their course toward the equator.

The inhabitants of these Islands, once happy and sequestered from the world, have preserved by tradition the history of their origin, but too indefinite and obscure to throw any light on the subject and serve the historian in tracing them back to any other country. Their Kahutee, which means 'the land of our fathers', will not, I believe, agree with the name of any other country from which they might have migrated. It may be a corruption of Otahute, but the distance between the two places would render at that distant period a communication improbable.

Be that as it may, nature has given them a Country rich in fruits, many of which are peculiar to itself, favourable to health and bodily strength, and not averse to indolence and pleasure, and the easy means to procure subsistence. But new wants, with new acquaintances, have originated and have been a drawback on their primitive pleasure, and may in the end produce an order of things, replete with more lasting happiness.

Monarchy, or despotism, has been the government of these Islands from time immemorial, and at present they all pay homage to Tamaahamaah, who from a king of one single district, Owyhee, has raised himself to the absolute sovereignty of the whole group excepting Attoi to the leeward.

The succession to the throne is hereditary, but the lineal descent is traced from the mother, though I have not heard of an instance where a woman has swayed the royal sceptre, although they have in the order of their nobility received the homage of the reigning Prince. These people are never heard to complain of the injustice, or rapacity of their kings, who have completely succeeded in depriving of them the right of property. The subject, in silence, himself depossesed of his estate, while it is given to a stranger, and at the same time entertaining the highest veneration for his sovereign, always proud of displaying the smallest instance of his favour.

It is not an easy matter in any country, to pierce the veil that covers the mysteries of religion, but as far as I have been able to penetrate, have found the religion of these Islanders simple and natural. Its rite and mysteries are entrusted solely to the Priests, who always perform with simple hands the sacerdotal duties. The exact number of their Gods, I have not been able to ascertain, nor the qualities and duties assigned them; they have undoubtedly many subordinate deities, but Oroono, as the name implies, is the highest of all their Gods, the first in power and goodness.

The Temple of the Gods is generally the constant abode of the Priests, who perform all the sacrifices, and present every offering. They believe in bribes, propitiation and expiation; hence the idea of sacrificing to the Gods, and whatever has been offered to the Gods can never be removed from the altar, which in all the old Morai's has become an immense pile of bones and rotten vegetables. The Morai is sacred to all but the Priest, the very railing of the enclosure cannot be touched with impunity, by any of the common people, or even the chiefs, unless they belong to the priesthood, so inviolate is held whatever appertains to the Gods.

I have never heard them speak of rewards or punishments in another world, the consequence of good or bad actions in this. The priest points out a happy hereafter, the unprohibited privilege of all who live, where felicity mixed with affliction awaits them in another world. They do not suppose that those pleasures will be of a celestial kind, but such as may be recognized and relished by the senses: eating, drinking and the enjoyment of natural pleasures; sickness, pain, and death have no admittance into their paradise of perfection. Where trees of delicious fruit, and leaves eternal shall enshadow the streams, all that can gratify and delight the senses, shall there be enjoyed without care, and without labour. Impressed with these happy ideas, there are no victims to despair; they are always easy, cheerful and gay.

Although there are no future rewards, or punishments, held forth in their religious creed, to encourage morality, or deter vice, yet there are as few crimes in society of a destructive nature among them as any other people.

From the imperfect knowledge I had of their language, I was never able to learn the particular powers assigned to their deities; but from circumstances, am led to believe they are very limited, excepting those of Oroono, the chief of all their gods, whose power is above all. To all the subordinate deities they present their offerings and address their prayers, as they suppose they need their assistance; and it often happens that when as they suppose their gifts and prayers have been rendered vain, and their faith disappointed, that they will pass the shrine of the unpropitious deity with evident signs of contempt. They do not suppose their powers to extend beyond the limits of natural things and only view them as temporal guardians. They deposit their dead on their Morais; almost every family having its own, in which is placed an image of their tutelary god, and are held sacred from all wanton violation, or vagrant intrusion. All offenses of this nature, before their acquaintance with foreigners, were punished with death, but instances of the kind were very seldom, so great was their veneration for these mysterious enclosures, which frequently stand in some remote and solitary part of their plantation.

The Priests have assigned to them a two-fold duty, not only the mysteries of religion, but the performance of all exterior rites; they keep the traditions of the country, and regulate the Calendar, and also preserve the laws of the land, which seem to be so interwoven with religion that it is not easy to separate them.

If a stranger should happen to approach near one of their Morais, with an apparent intention to enter, the Priest will tell him, it is "Taboo'd" that is, interdicted: this term "taboo" is so very indefinite, that I have been led to believe that it has very extensive and important meanings. All temporary laws of the King are called taboos; the Seasons, or divisions of the years, are marked by taboos; all religious interdictions, of whatever kind, are called taboos; all the annual festivals are likewise called taboos; and, it is by a regular routine of these taboos, each consisting of a certain number of days, with known intervals between, that the Priest is enabled to announce the beginning and end of a year.

The Year begins with the new Moon happening about October, and when thirteen moons have passed away, the year is then ended. There always being a certain number of days to be set apart as a taboo, and celebrated as an annual festival. By this method they are able to bring the year about with tolerable accuracy.

Manners and Customs

It was the opinion of those who first visited these islands that the inhabitants were cannibals; and they had much reason for that belief, in the affair of Capt. Cook. But under happier auspices and a more extensive knowledge of their language, assisted by those who have resided many years with them, I am enabled to contradict a report, so injurious to a sequestered, though generous people. In a conversation I had with some of the natives, who accompanied us to the northwest coast of America in 1805, they appeared to be struck with horror at the imputation of such practices, and asked if that was the custom with us.

Mr. Young, who has resided with them for more than twenty years, told me that it never was a popular custom with them to offer up human sacrifice to the Gods of the country, and happening but once during his residence among them. At the close of the war, carried on by the present sovereign against the rival chiefs, an offering was made at the Morai of Tocaigh, of twelve men slain in battle, five hundred hogs, and three thousand plantains and bananas. Not an instance happening through the whole course of the war was a prisoner sacrificed to satiate the appetite of man, or discharge a duty to their Gods.

They are docile, and obedient to their superiors, brave and patient in war; and indolent in prosperity, addicted to gaming, particularly among the chiefs, who generally have the most leisure. I have seen the men and women sitting for hours together, playing at a kind of checquers. They have also many other sedentary games. But they are most fond of the athletic game, and dancing, with which they celebrate their great festivals, where it is not infrequently seen that men, women and children engage with each other in feats of boxing, in which they always preserve their temper, never suffering themselves to be carried away by passion or revenge.

Their dances, which are generally performed in large and open areas, admit of great numbers joining in them, their motions are all correspondent and regular. Every performer chants a part of the music to which they all move, but the principal singers stand in the front line of the performers and give notice of the intended song. On these occasions their dress is elegant and fancyful. Some of the ornaments, after the dance is over, are deposited in the Morai. From this circumstance, I have been led to believe that there is something of religion blended with festivity. No pains are spared on these occasions to appear well dressed. I have seen two elderly women attentively employed for a half an hour in dressing a young beauty for a courtly ball, for it was by order of the King they were to assemble. Although the general motion, or figure of their dances, is not so intricate as those with us, they are performed with the greatest possible harmony.

Marriage is not, perhaps, by these people held to be so sacred a tie as with us, although a violation of its rites is punishable according to the laws or usage of the country. Parties may separate, at anytime, by mutual agreement, as neither priest nor magistrate are called upon to sanction or consecrate the union. In such cases where children have been the fruit of an alliance, they are generally divided, the mother taking the female part of the family, when it happens that children of both sexes compose it, and the father the sons.

The punishment of adultery is burning the house of the offending party, when the injured husband chooses to avail himself of that custom, which is the law of the land, and is assisted in the execution of it by his friends and relations, without the aid of the magistrate. The husband may kill the party, when he happens to be surprised in the act, in or about his own house and enclosures. The husband may, with or without the consent of his wife, sell her to a neighbor; but instances of this kind are not plenty. The present King of Attoi is a living example of this barter of wives, the favourite queen having been purchased from a chief of the Island.

In no country, I believe, is the indulgence of natural desires so common as here; yet that dreadful attendant on promiscuous enjoyment which has marked its way through other countries, was a stranger here until introduced by the first visitors. That this disorder should never have made its appearance, may be owing to the habit of bathing, an institution supported both by laws and religion, but more particularly by the soft, though irresistible allurements of Nature, and is the particular amusement of both sexes. They are, in this useful and pleasant exercise, expert in the extreme. Although I have visited these Islands several times, yet I have never heard of an instance of any person drowning, though they have frequently been upset in their canoes at great distance from the shore.

I once saw an incident in Karakakooa Bay, when our Ship was surrounded by a great number of the natives of all ages and sexes, some in canoes, but a far greater number without, of several girls being upset in a canoe, who appeared in no way alarmed by the accident. One of them very coolly collected the paddles and furniture of the canoe together, while the others turned it on its bottom again, and placing themselves on each side of it, by an ingenious and happy effort, gave it a gentle motion at first, to and fro, which soon became violent, then checking it on a sudden, when the water which it contained shot out of each end. By repeating the operation two or three times, the canoe was discharged of its water, and they again seated themselves in it without exciting the notice of their neighbors.

Mr. Young, who has had a great opportunity for observation, having generally partaken of their toils and amusements, told me that he never knew an instance wherein they complained of being tired in swimming, but that they sometimes did of being cold. I have seen the children like shoals of porpoises playing and diverting themselves in the billows dashed on the beach, under the care and direction of some domestic of the family. Thus early habituated to combat the waves, they are enabled through life to meet all accidents of that nature with coolness and the full use of their faculties. To prevent injury to the skin by too frequently bathing in salt water, they will invariably wash themselves down in freshwater. And in all situations where fresh water can be had in bodies sufficiently large for swimming and bathing in, it is always preferred.

APPENDIX

Agriculture forms the greatest part of their employment, and is managed by the middle-aged and elderly classes of society, the elderly women generally sharing the labour of the field with the men. Young people and children seldom labour unless it be for amusement; young and unmarried women never.

The wealthier sort of the inhabitants use both animal and vegetable food, and are particularly fond of salted pork and fish dried. Salt is an indispensable article with them, and is produced in abundance by evaporation, and is profusely used at their meals, particularly of fresh fish, which they prefer raw. Their method of cooking is baking or steaming underground, with vegetables which they afterwards knead into a pudding, or paste, and dilute it with water as they like best. This preparation they call "Poie", which after undergoing a moderate fermentation, is both pleasant and nutritive. Strangers soon become fond of it, and many have acknowledged its excellent qualities in restoring to the stomach its proper tone, and repairing injured constitutions.

There are several kinds of animal, as vegetable, food which the women are not permitted to use. They may eat fowls, but not their eggs, they cannot eat pork without a violation of the Taboo, which formerly was, and I believe at present, punished by death. Coconuts and Plantains are also prohibited. Of this palpable injustice, and inequality, I never heard a complaint. The flesh of dogs forms the greatest part of the animal food consumed by the women, and the men of all conditions are fond of it.

The men and women never eat together, always having separate houses for that purpose, which in their language are called "eating houses."

They have long been acquainted with advantages arising from watering their grounds. Many of their works for this purpose reflect great credit on their talents and industry. Their plantations generally lie along the banks of the rivers and brooks, out of which the water is led in small channels through all the plain, branching off in different directions, intersecting each other, and dividing the whole plain into small plantations, which are always kept moist by the small streams surrounding them.

The Tarrah, one of the most nutritious vegetables in the world, requires in its growth perpetual inundation. To effect this, they raise a bank, or dyke, round the area intended for its vegetation, so tight as to prevent the water from running off, after which they plant the Tarrah, and inundate the whole enclosure to a depth of about 12or 14 inches.

The method of planting the Tarrah is cutting the root towards the top, so that their will be a sufficient portion to germinate, and no further care is wanted.

I have seen on the Island of Attoi, canals for the purpose of watering the lands, which were elevated 40 or 50 feet above the bed of the river, and separated from other plains which lay farther up by vast ridges of rocks.

The river in its passage round this promontory having descended 50 or 60 feet, in a distance of half a mile, formed by raising a wall of stone from the bed of the river, round this promontory to a height sufficient to carry the water in a uniform line on to the plain below. Upon the top of this wall a trench was constructed and tightened with clay, or other adhesive matter, so as to retain the water insufficient quantities to water many hundred acres.

Production of the soil:
There are but few fruits on these Islands but what are common to other tropical countries. The bread fruit, which grows on trees smaller than the sycamore, and big as a shaddock, filled with a farinaceous or pulpy substance; and the Tie, a root, exquisitely sweet and delightful to the taste after being baked in the earth. From this root the natives, by the assistance of some foreigners residing among them, make a strong distilled liquor, resembling in taste and smell, indifferent gin.

APPENDIX

The Ava, or Rava, which they cultivate with considerable care for its root, which has the peculiar property of intoxicating and producing sleep. They chew the root and afterward express the juice, which they drink with their meals in the evening. There may be some medical properties in this root. The foreigners residing here say that it is a certain cure for the venereal disease. But certain it is that it has rendered the skins of those dry and scaly who have indulged in a long and immoderate use of it. They have a powerful vegetable emetic, the name of which I am not acquainted. Notwithstanding the opinion of Mr. Anderson, who accompanied Captain Cook, to the contrary, this fact is well known to several navigators. To Capt. Jonathan Winship of Boston I am indebted for the information.

The Tarrah, an esculent or edible root, I believe is frequently found in other tropical countries, but not in such perfection as here, where it is cultivated with uncommon care, and forms a principal part of their food.

APPENDIX

Yams, Plantains, and Potatoes are common to all tropical countries, and are found here in abundance. The Orange which begins to flourish here is an exotic from the coast of Peru. So are Maize, Pumpkins, Melons, Cabbages, and Tobacco, which grow to the greatest perfection. Turnips, Radishes and Onions are also foreigners.

The Ahua, the apple tree of these Islands, is pleasant and juicy, lightly mingled with acid, of the size of a small Peach, with a small stone or kernel.

The Tootooe, I believe, is also a native of these and some other south sea Islands, and is a tree resembling the Tamarind in shape and size. It bears a nut somewhat like the walnut with a rich oily kernel, frequently eaten by the natives, and not unpleasant in its taste. But it is more valuable for the oil they extract from it, with which they mix their paints and the shell, when burnt to a cinder and ground fine, is their only black paint. This oil will not leave so fine a gloss on paint work as linseed, but is very durable. The people gather these nuts before the shell becomes hard, and string them on long, fine skewers, and when they become well dried, burn them in the evening to light their houses.

The Tappa, or cloth tree, is to them the most valuable, and is planted and tended with great care. The grounds appropriated for its growth, unless naturally defended, are enclosed on the East with a high wicker fence, thatched with leaves of the plantain, 18 or 20 feet, to defend it from the morning sun, and perhaps from the easterly wind. The ground is kept clean and free from a weeds and shrubs. So injurious is the sun, or easterly wind to this plant that next to the wall the shoots are tall and vigorous, and the leaves of a dark and thrifty green, degenerating regularly in size and color toward the western part of the area. From the bark of this tree, they make all their clothes, by a process similar to that of paper making, and is by oiling and glazing rendered very durable. They likewise paint and stain it in very beautiful and brilliant colours. This tree is undoubtedly a species of the paper Mulberry.

Sandal wood, of an indifferent kind, is found in the interior of the Islands, and has frequently been carried to China, but has never rewarded the adventurer; but in a late trial, by selecting the best quality, is likely to succeed at least so far as to pay the freight.

They have several other kinds of wood, some of which will answer for Ship timber, and others for Cabinet work, particularly the Hammer, of a fine curly grain.

The Sugarcane, which they call Hokah, is a native of the Islands, and to a greater size than I have seen in any other country, and will in the course of time supply with sugar, and rum, the settlements which will be made on the northwest shores of America.

They have many other shrubs and trees which are used for various purposes. The Ahalla, the branches of which bear an overgrown proportion to the trunk, its leaves resembling those of Flag or

Callimus. Its fruit resembles the pineapple, and its rind is covered with protuberances, regularly arranged, of about the size of an acorn, and when ripe, of a beautiful yellow. The women frequently cut and string them like beads, and wear them on their heads and necks by way of ornament.

The Oranah is a shrub used in dyeing a beautiful yellow; the root when properly prepared makes a good curry, and is perhaps the same substance from which curry is made in other countries.

Harrah is likewise a shrub which grows in straight shoots to the height of 3 or 4 feet. This plant is poison, or it has the singular property of intoxication, and is used ingeniously by the inhabitants for the purpose of fishing. This is done by bruising the plant till its juice can readily be mixed with the water into which it is thrown. They then proceed to sea, keeping the shore in sight until they fall in with a shoal of fish. The harrah is then thrown into the water, round about the fish, and in a few minutes many of them are seen floating on their sides deprived of life and motion, and are immediately taken into the canoe.

Nunnee: this shrub is reared from the seed, and is planted in the their cultivated grounds. They make from its root a beautiful red dye with which they stain their cloth.

Miah: a species of the Plantain is the banana.

Tooh is a tree, the lower part of the trunk and root of which the natives use to make their trays, and other culinary utensils. Its trunk is crooked, and short, with large spreading branches and leaves resembling the poplar, very proper for shade and generally grown near the houses. They have not at present got the apple, the peach of Europe, all attempts to introduce them having failed.

Persons of the Natives

The men are generally above the common size, well limbed, and fleshy, though never so fat and corpulent as to render them clumsy and unwieldy. The young and middle aged, with but few exceptions, are handsome, with strong black hair and beards. They formerly cut their hair close on the sides of the head, leaving it long on the top extending from the forehead to the back of the head, and always going bareheaded. Their skin of a dark copper colour, by being always exposed to the sun, and often to the salt water, has become with the elderly peoples coarse and hard. I never saw but few instances of deformity among them, and their diseases are generally fevers, and complaints of the head, and frequently among the younger people cutaneous eruptions.

Situated as they are between the tropics, it would be natural to suppose they could not stand the cold of higher latitudes. We had six of these men employed onboard the Ship, during the time on the northwest coast of America, a period of sixteen months. We passed the winter between the parallels of 55 degrees and 56 degrees of north Lat'de, and in all instances they were known to perform their duty with as little complaint as any of our seamen, several of whom were natives of the north of Europe.

Whether they were stimulated to this from motives of personal honor, or national pride, I cannot say; but both perhaps had some small agency in prompting their exertions. It may also depend on bodily constitution and the texture of the skin, which renders them impervious to the cold. There is something in the texture of their skin widely different from the inhabitants of Africa, and their descendants in America, who in all their exercise sweat freely, and at all times emit an unpleasant smell. This, however, is not the case with these islanders, they do not perspire so freely, neither is there anything offensive in their smell.

The women in general are not so handsome, I think, as the men; neither are they so tall and slender as the females of the South of Europe, or their descendants in the United States, yet there are some elegant figures among them, and a low degree of deformity than can, perhaps, be found in any other country. Their limbs are perfect and show at once a just symmetry; their features are regular, though not so acute as the French or Italians; their teeth are clean and beautiful in the fullest sense of the word; their eyes, though not small, want the clearness and vivacity of the people last mentioned, and are always dark, marked with full fine veins. Their hair is strong, black and bushy, when permitted to grow, but by an elegant and prevailing custom, it is kept quite short, which adds both to beauty and to health. They reach the years of puberty much sooner than they do in Europe or America, but are not fond of becoming mothers and taking upon themselves the care of families. We have generally observed that the middle aged women have been burdened with young children, yet they are kind and indulgent to their living children. Size and corpulence in the women are thought to be by the men a criterion of beauty, and are almost invariably found in the families of the chiefs.

These people cannot be persuaded to depart from the religious and civic institutions of their ancestors, yet they are docile and teachable to a very sensible degree, and have already with a lucky facility adopted some of the useful arts of other countries, and have given strong proofs of their industry and imitative powers. Although they were enabled with their own native implement, before their intercourse with foreigners, to finish their canoes, spears and household utensils with great neatness, yet they have given a decided preference to our iron tools, and use them on all occasions.

The present King has already discovered from his intercourse with foreigners, particularly the Americans, the value and use of money, and has already adopted a system of finance, in order to collect into his own coffer the small quantities of cash left on the Island by foreigners. His knowledge as a financier is very extensive, for although he is determined to have all the money on the Island, yet his mode of collecting is mild and sure of success.

With this revenue, in the course of a few years, he has been able to purchase a Ship of two hundred tons. I saw her in 1806; she was hauled upon the beach, and had undergone a thorough repair, having been sheathed with the materials of the Islands, and is now waiting to collect from the trading ships a sufficient quantity of copper nails and sheet copper to complete her bottom. He has likewise 18 or 20 small schooners built partly by his own people and partly by the foreigners residing among them. Capt. Vancouver, in 1794, laid the keel and set up the frame of the *Tamanah*, a schooner of about 18 or 20 tons, which was afterwards finished by some white men in the King's employ. From that time, his people began the study of naval architecture and have been progressing toward perfection in a degree unequaled by any other people in their first efforts towards civilization and the arts.

I think it not improbable that His present Pacific Majesty, for so I shall call him, will in the course of a few years attempt a commercial intercourse with the Russian or Russi, an American Company established at Norfolk Sound, in which he may supply them with Beef, Pork and Vegetables, and at no distant time with Sugar and rum. He has already, from the stock which Capt. Vancouver left with him, an abundant stock of cattle, and pork has ever been the principal animal food of the Islands. They manufacture an excellent kind of cordage suitable for the running rigging of ships, from the bark of a tree, also small line from a species of hemp, equal to anything I have ever seen of the kind. Tobacco may also become an article of trade.

Traditionary Accounts, taken from some of the best informed residents on the Islands:
The Priests have preserved an account of their origin and say: that many years ago, beyond their power to enumerate, that Kahinu and Mowee came in a Canoe to the Island of Awyhu, and landed on its eastern part. They brought with them Hogs, Dogs, and domestic Fowls, and it does not appear that there were any other domestic or wild animals on these Islands when first discovered by the English.

The Priests say that in the time of Kahinu and Mowee that the vegetables of the Islands were so scarce that it was with the greatest difficulty they obtained the means to subsist on them. This sterility was undoubtedly occasioned by the frequent eruptions from the volcanoes which kept the face of the country covered with a thick lava. The people have a story among them, that in the time of this great scarcity, mother Mowee ordered a fire to be kindled at the entrance of a cave on the shore, descending to an unknown depth; and that after the fire had begun to burn briskly, she passed through it, and entered the cave, and afterwards returned byway of the sea, bringing with her a large quantity of fish in a net, which she wore after the manner of an apron, sufficient to relieve their present distress, and with the power of ever after supplying their wants. Mr. Young, who related this story to me, has frequently seen the cave.

The country from which Kahinu and Mowee migrated they call Kahutee, which now in their language signifies 'the Land of our Fathers'. But where this land is situated they do not pretend to say. The only people they resemble is the Malays or Indians, and from those, in some anterior age, they undoubtedly descended and under the present arrangement of the Globe and the situation of the Islands in the South Pacific Ocean, I am led to believe that the Friendly Islands, or the Marquesas, is their celebrated Kahutee.

While laying at Karakakooa Bay, I took a trip over to the place where the celebrated Capt. Cook was killed. It is a small village on the northwest arm of the Bay of Karakakooa. I was not able to discover any trace of the affair from the trees being marked with shot. The Priests and intelligent people of the Island told Mr. Young that Capt. Cook was received and honored as a God, and that his person was viewed as sacred; but after his taking the consecrated fence which surrounded the Morai, and converting it into fuel for his Ships, and on their part, the stealing one of his boats, and the death of one of the chiefs in his attempt to regain his boat, prompted them to lift their hands against him and revenge the injury. This resolution was not general, for many through fear, or affection, endeavored to divert the brother of him who was slain. They always view this affair, perhaps, in a proper light and have ever regretted the deed, always charging the English with being the aggressors, thus justifying themselves for retaliating the death of a respectable countryman.

BIBLIOGRAPHY

Allen, Oliver. *The Pacific Navigators.* Alexandria, VA: Time-Life Books, 1980.

Bancroft, H. H. *History of the Northwest Coast.* Vol. II, 1800-1846. San Francisco: The History Company, 1886.

Barrow, Sir John, *A Description of Pitcairn's Island and its Inhabitants. With Authentic Account of the Mutiny of the Ship Bounty.* . . New York: Harper & Brothers, 1838.

Beaglehole, John Cawte. *Life of Captain James Cook.* Stanford: Stanford University Press, 1974.

Brodie, Walter. *Pitcairn's Island and the Islanders, in 1850* . . . Second edition. London: Whittaker & Co., 1851.

Bryan, William A. *Natural History of Hawaii* . . . Honolulu: Hawaii Gazette, 1915.

BIBLIOGRAPHY

Collett, Bill. *The Last Mutiny*. New York: W. W. Norton, 1995.

Cutler, Carl C. *Important Types of Merchant Sailing Craft*. Mystic, Conn.: Marine Historical Association, 1958.

Dana, Richard Henry. *Two Years Before the Mast*. New York: Harper & Brothers, 1840.

Davis, Charles G. (Illustrator). *Rigs of the Nine Principal Types of American Sailing Vessels*. Salem, Mass.: Peabody Museum, 1981.

Fairburn, William Armstrong. *Merchant Sail*. Vol. I, II. Center Lovell, Maine: Fairburn Marine Education Foundation, 1955.

Feher, Joseph (compiler). *Hawaii: A Pictorial History*. Honolulu: Bishop Museum Press, 1969.

Gibson, James R. *Otter Skins, Boston Ships, and China Goods: The Maritime Fur Trade of the Northwest Coast, 1785-1841*. Seattle: University of Washington Press, 1992.

Hawks, David Freeman. *Everyday Life in Early America*. New York: Harper and Rowe, 1988.

Heilprin, Angelo, and Louis Heilprin (editors). *Geographical Dictionary of the World ...* Philadelphia and London: J. B. Lippincott, [1918?].

BIBLIOGRAPHY

Hough, Richard. *The Last Voyage of Captain James Cook.* New York: William Morrow, 1979.

Howay, F. W. *A List of the Trading Vessels in the Maritime Fur Trade, 1785-1825.* Edited by Richard A. Pierce. Kingston, Ontario: The Limestone Press, 1973.

Kirker, James. *Adventures to China: Americans in the Southern Oceans, 1792-1812.* New York: Oxford University Press, 1970.

Lomask, Milton. *The Biographer's Craft.* New York: Harper and Rowe, 1986.

Lower, J. Arthur. *Ocean of Destiny: A Concise History of the North Pacific, 1500-1978.* Vancouver: University of British Columbia Press, 1978.

McLean, Alistair. *Captain Cook.* Garden City, New York: Doubleday, 1972.

Malloy, Mary. *"Boston Men" on the Northwest Coast: The American Maritime Fur Trade, 1788-1844.* Kingston, Ontario, and Fairbanks, Alaska: The Limestone Press, 1998.

Morison, S. E. *The Maritime History of Massachusetts, 1783-1860.* Boston: Northeastern University Press, 1979.

BIBLIOGRAPHY

Ogden, Adele. *The California Sea Otter Trade, 1784-1848.* Berkeley: University of California Press, 1941.

Paluka, Frank. *The Three Voyages of Captain Cook.* Pittsburg: Beta Phi Mu, 1974.

Patterson, Samuel. *Narrative of the Adventures and Sufferings of Samuel Patterson . . .* Fairfield, Washington: Ye Galleon Press, 1967.

Porter, David. *Journal of a Cruise.* Annapolis: Naval Institute Press, 1986.

Reynolds, Stephen. *Voyage of the New Hazard to the Northwest Coast, Hawaii and China, 1810-1813.* Edited by F. W. Howay. Fairfield, Washington: Ye Galleon Press, 1970.

Ross, Frank E. American Adventures in Early Marine Fur Trade with China. Reprint from *Chinese Social and Political Science Review*, Vol. 21, no. 2, July 1937.

Sargent, Charles L. *The Life of Alexander Smith . . .* Boston: Sylvester T. Goss, 1819.

Scofield, John. *Hail, Columbia! Robert Gray, John Kendrick, and the Pacific Fur Trade.* Portland: Oregon Historical Society Press, 1992.

BIBLIOGRAPHY

Shillibeer, John. *A Narrative of the Briton's Voyage, to Pitcairn's Island.* London: Law and Whittaker, 1817.

Ship Registers of the District of Boston, MA, 1811-1820. The National Archives Project, 1939.

Sturgis, William. *A Most Remarkable Enterprise: Maritime Commerce and Culture on the Northwest Coast.* Edited, with an introduction and commentary, by Mary Malloy. Hyannis, Mass.: Pinnace Press, 1997.

Tavernier, Bruno. *Great Maritime Routes: An Illustrated History.* Translated by Nicholas Fry. New York: Viking Press, 1972.

Terrell, John Upton. *Furs by Astor.* New York: William Morrow, 1963.

Villiers, Alan. *Men, Ships and the Sea.* Washington: National Geographic Society, 1962.

Manuscripts

Log of the *Pearl*, microfilm, Massachusetts Historical Society, Boston.

Caleb Reynolds, *Collected manuscripts*, 1771-1858.

BIBLIOGRAPHY

Solid Men of Boston in the Northwest, microfilm, William Dane Phelps, Bancroft Library, University of California, Berkeley.

INDEX

(Ships are listed together under "Vessels.")

INDEX

Vessels

INDEX

INDEX

Swallow, H.M.S., Carteret, 88
Taber, Sole, 164
Tagus, H.M.S., Pipon, 89
Tamanah,194
Topaz, Folger, 88, 89, 130
Traveller, Wilcocks, 125
Union, 139
Volunteer, 69
Zephyr, Brintnall, 73

Walker, capt., *King George*, 82
War of 1812, 45
Wetmore, William S., 138, 148
Whampoa, 23, 116, 120, 123
Whittemore, Isaac, capt., mate, 99; *Avon*, 43, 67, 99-100, 101; death of, 101-102, 104-105, 112
Wilcocks, capt., *Traveller*, 125
Williams, Mary, 46-47, 52-53
Williams, Lydia, 46
Williams, Nathaniel, 46
Williams, Richard, 48

Williams, Seth, 53
Williams, Thomas, 158
Winship, capt., *O'Cain*, 21, 34; *Albatross*, 34
Winship, Jonathan, 31, 33, 184
Winship, Nathan, 31, 70, 74
Winship brothers, 34, 37, 38, 42

Young, John, 12, 13, 21, 22-23, 107, 108, 133, 174, 179, 197

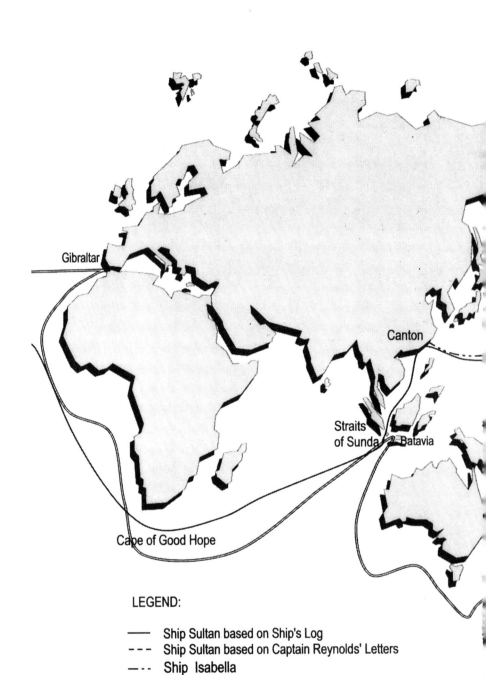

Gibraltar

Canton

Straits
of Sunda   Batavia

Cape of Good Hope

LEGEND:

——— Ship Sultan based on Ship's Log
- - - Ship Sultan based on Captain Reynolds' Letters
—·· Ship Isabella
══ Ship Fame